KARL BARTH

Makers of the Modern Theological Mind

Bob E. Patterson, Editor

Makers of the Modern Theological Mind
Bob E. Patterson, Editor

KARL
BARTH

by David L. Mueller

HENDRICKSON
PUBLISHERS
PEABODY, MASSACHUSETTS 01961-3473

KARL BARTH

Copyright © 1972
Hendrickson Publishers, Inc.
P.O. Box 3473
Peabody, Massachusetts 01961–3473
All rights reserved.
Printed in the United States of America

ISBN 0–943575–55–9

To
Marilyn
and
Charles and Mary Thompson

The following abbreviations are used to refer to some of Barth's writings:

C.D.   *Church Dogmatics*
K.D.   *Kirchliche Dogmatik*

Contents

7

Editor's Preface

Who are the thinkers that have shaped Christian theology in our time? This series tries to answer that question by providing a reliable guide to the ideas of the men who have significantly charted the theological seas of our century. In the current revival of theology, these books will give a new generation the opportunity to be exposed to significant minds. They are not meant, however, to be a substitute for a careful study of the original works of these makers of the modern theological mind.

This series is not for the lazy. Each major theologian is examined carefully and critically—his life, his theological method, his most germinal ideas, his weaknesses as a thinker, his place in the theological spectrum, and his chief contribution to the climate of theology today. The books are written with the assumption that laymen will read them and enter into the theological dialogue that is so necessary to the church as a whole. At the same time they are carefully enough designed to give assurance to a Ph.D. student in theology preparing for his preliminary exams.

Each author in the series is a professional scholar and theologian in his own right. All are specialists on, and in some cases have studied with, the theologians about whom they write. Welcome to the series.

BOB E. PATTERSON, Editor
Baylor University

Preface

During the period from 1932 to 1967 Barth published thirteen volumes of his *Church Dogmatics* totaling over 9000 pages in German! Obviously, it is quite presumptuous to write a "brief introduction" to the thought of a theologian who may be called a modern "Church Father." Nevertheless, the attempt has been made. Whether the most important things which ought to go into such an introduction have been said and whether the analysis is reliable are for others to judge.

It is not possible to survey the entire *Church Dogmatics* in one small volume. Therefore, after an analysis of Barth's early development, major attention is accorded the doctrine of revelation, which bears upon everything else Barth writes. The third chapter is an analysis of some aspects of Barth's christocentric theology. The conclusion is an assessment of both some of the strengths and weaknesses of Barth's theology.

Throughout, it is my intention to interpret Barth fairly. Numerous quotations are used in order to provide the reader with something of the flavor of Barth's method and style. In most instances, I have used the official English translation of the *Church Dogmatics*. Though I have profited from reading some of Barth's critics, limitations of space precluded much dialogue with them. A Protestant, Thomas F. Torrance, and a Roman Catholic, Hans Urs von Balthasar, have been the most helpful interpreters of Barth with respect to his theological method and the transitions in his pilgrimage. My hope is that this work will whet the reader's appetite to the extent that he will read Barth on his own.

My father, William A. Mueller, was the first to introduce me to Barth's thought. In the early thirties, he wrote a doctoral dissertation dealing with the dialectical theology of the early Barth; some twenty-five years later (1958), I completed a doctoral dissertation at Duke University dealing with Barth's theological method. During the year 1959–60, I took a leave of absence from Baylor University in order to pursue post-graduate studies at the University of Basel in Switzerland. I am indebted to the J. Newton Rayzor Foundation for providing a grant which helped make that venture possible. The courtesies which Professor Barth extended me and the frequent contacts with him which seminars and colloquia made possible during that year will not be forgotten.

This book is dedicated to three people who shared in the joys of that year in Basel. Mr. and Mrs. Charles E. Thompson, my wife's parents, visited us in Basel and shared in the excitement which marked participation in one of the English colloquia chaired by the grand "old man" of Basel, Karl Barth. My wife Marilyn enriched the time we spent together in Basel and our common pilgrimage in the intervening years.

A special word of thanks is due friends who assisted me in this project. Mr. Warren McWilliams typed and corrected a rough draft of this manuscript. Miss Jean Aiken, office services supervisor, and her staff typed the final draft. Dr. Ronald F. Deering, associate librarian, read the manuscript and gave me helpful counsel.

DAVID L. MUELLER

I. Karl Barth:
His Life and Thought
(1886-1968)

HIS LIFE AND INFLUENCE

The life and work of Karl Barth were as rich and full as his multivolumed *Church Dogmatics*, the most comprehensive interpretation of the Christian faith in modern theology. With his death in his birthplace, Basel, Switzerland, at the age of eighty-two, the Christian church lost one of its most learned, colorful, and devoted teachers.

Barth is generally regarded as a modern "church father" who belongs in the list of the most illustrious theologians in the history of Christianity. Future generations will not hesitate to speak of him with Augustine and Aquinas, Luther and Calvin, and with Schleiermacher and Ritschl. Indeed, it is fair to say that even as Schleiermacher dominated the theology of the nineteenth century and is the father of liberal theology, so Barth dominated much of the theology of the twentieth century and is the father of neoreformation theology. What is more, his stature has been acclaimed both by Roman Catholic and Protestant interpreters. Yet perhaps the clearest testimony to Barth's monumental achievement in changing the direction of Protestant theology in this century as he moved "against the stream" of established patterns of thought is the fact that even his severest critics must establish their theological positions with respect to his.

THE EARLY YEARS, 1886–1909

What kind of theologian and man was Karl Barth? Although a brief biographical sketch cannot supply us with simple answers to questions about his greatness and influence, a review of some significant events in his life and pilgrimage may help to see him in historical perspective.

Karl Barth was born in Basel, Switzerland, on May 10, 1886, the first son of Fritz Barth, a minister of the Swiss Reformed Church and a teacher in the Evangelical School of Preachers in Basel. Both of Barth's grandfathers were also ministers. His father was a native of Basel. Some have traced certain of Barth's traits to the characteristics of the people of the German-speaking region of Switzerland and of his ancestry. He was marked by an unusual intellect, a great capacity for work, seriousness of purpose, a democratic spirit, an appreciation for the arts—especially music—and finally, by a wry and engaging sense of humor. Basel, where Barth died on December 10, 1968, was his home until the age of three and again from 1935 until his death. To live in Basel, says one writer, "means life in an ancient but now very modern, middle-sized, industrial, and university city, located on the Rhine where France, Germany, and Switzerland meet, as clean and sedate and beflowered and proud as a city can be." [1]

It is noteworthy that Barth's roots lie deeply imbedded in the Reformed or Calvinistic wing of the Swiss Reformation. When he was three years old, his father accepted a call to become a lecturer and subsequently a professor of Church History and New Testament Exegesis at the University of Bern. The academic and religious nurture of the Barth home must have exerted considerable influence. Peter, one of Karl's brothers, became the coeditor of a critical edition of Calvin's works. Another brother, Heinrich, became a reputable philosopher and served with his brother Karl on the faculty of the University of Basel until his retirement in 1960. It was in Bern, the capital of Switzerland, that Barth grew up and received his early religious training and formal education.

Parental guidance, his father's conservative theological position, and the influence of the Christian community account both for the fact that his "faith was nourished in positive evangelical theology" and for his appreciation of "sacred scholarship in the service of the Gospel."[2]

Late in life Barth recalled that his appetite for theology was first whetted through instruction related to his confirmation at the age of sixteen. It seemed to him a challenge not only to be able to know and affirm the Confessions of the church, but also to be able "to understand them from within." The pursuit of this goal made Barth resolve to become a theologian at the time of his confirmation.[3]

During his early schooling, Barth was interested in history and drama, whereas mathematics and the sciences held little attraction for him. This is why Arnold Come speaks of a bent in the young Barth which helps explain his subsequent "emphasis upon the Word of God as action, as event. He never became interested in pure research abstracted from life, even in the fields of exegesis and theology."[4]

Following the European custom which prevails to the present, Barth pursued his theological training in several universities. At eighteen years of age, he began his studies at the University of Bern. There he was most influenced by the thought of his father. In addition, he studied systematic theology under Herman Lüdemann, a rather influential theologian in the liberal tradition. The most significant event in Barth's intellectual pilgrimage at Bern occurred during the fourth semester, when he encountered both Kant's philosophy and Schleiermacher's theology. This intellectual liberation made Barth anxious to pursue his theological training with Wilhelm Herrmann of Marburg, the leading neo-Kantian theologian of the day. However, his father's desire that he study with a more conservative theologian led them to compromise on the University of Berlin where Barth spent the fall semester of 1906. This move was important not only because it marked the beginning of Barth's exposure to the reigning school of theological liberalism, but also because it afforded him close

contact with one of its last and most influential exponents in
the twentieth century, namely, Adolf von Harnack, the re-
nowned church historian.

Barth devoted himself so completely to his seminar work
with Harnack on "The Acts of the Apostles" that he gave only
passing attention to the lectures of Karl Holl, Julius Kaftan,
and Hermann Gunkel. Indeed, Barth later confessed that he
was so absorbed in his studies that he failed to take advantage
of Berlin's cultural riches. Nor did he become Harnack's
disciple! The young theolog of twenty, though impressed with
Harnack's erudition, found the latter's version of the gospel
set forth in his famous Heidelberg lectures of 1899–1900
entitled *The Essence of Christianity* to be a form of cultural
Christianity. He was drawn ever more strongly to Marburg
and Herrmann through reading the latter's *Ethics*. In the year
1925, Barth said: "The day twenty years ago in Berlin when
I first read his *Ethik* . . . I remember as if it were today."[5]
But in deference to his father's wishes, he returned to study
at Bern in the summer of 1907. In the fall of 1907, he en-
rolled at Tübingen to study for a semester with Adolph
Schlatter, a rather well-known conservative Swiss New Testament theologian. Barth was not greatly impressed with
Schlatter, and he seems to have spent more time working in
systematic theology with Theodor Häring.

Barth's desire to study with Herrmann at Marburg was
realized in the fall of 1908. He spent three semesters listening
to Herrmann, whom he later referred to as *"the* theological
teacher of my student years."[6] Although Barth also said on
the same occasion that he became a somewhat "surprising
disciple of Herrmann" in saying things "quite differently"
from his mentor, he concluded: ". . . I could never inwardly
agree that I had really turned away from my teacher."[7] In the
light of Barth's subsequent theological development, one may
interpret the latter remark to refer to Barth's continuing
appreciation for the christological focus of his "unforgettable
teacher."

While at Marburg, Barth also pursued his interest in Kant

through study with the leading neo-Kantian philosophers of the day, Hermann Cohen and Paul Natorp. In addition, he continued his biblical studies with the eminent New Testament theologians Johannes Weiss, Wilhelm Heitmüller, and Adolf Jülicher. It was soon to become apparent, however, that Barth was not satisfied with a purely historical-critical understanding of the biblical text which did not come to grips with its subject matter. This was the charge he later made against some of the liberal biblical scholars who dominated the discipline of biblical studies during his student days.

Barth concluded his formal theological education at Marburg at the age of twenty-three. After completing the theological examinations set by the Church of Bern in 1909, he was ordained. However, he never pursued doctoral studies in theology. After having made his mark theologically, numerous institutions gladly accorded him their highest honorary degrees.

TRANSITION TO DIALECTICAL THEOLOGY, 1909-1922

Upon the completion of his examinations and ordination, Barth did not feel quite ready to assume pastoral duties. This was due, in part, to Herrmann's repeated emphasis that all true preaching must grow out of the experience of the proclaimer. Since Barth did not feel that he possessed such deep religious experience, he chose instead to return to Marburg in order to serve as an assistant to Martin Rade, the editor of *Christliche Welt*, an influential liberal periodical which concentrated upon the church's responsibility in the world. Barth's growing ethical sensitivity concerning the mission of the church in society was deepened by this brief apprenticeship.

Later in 1909, Barth returned to his homeland in order to begin his pastoral ministry as an apprentice pastor of the German-speaking Reformed Church of Geneva, Switzerland, where he remained until 1911. The frame of mind in which Barth assumed his pastoral duties is evident in an article pub-

lished in 1909. The thesis Barth sets forth is that the theological graduates of the more liberal faculties of Marburg and
Heidelberg are more reluctant to enter into practical forms of
church work (pastoral, missionary, etc.) than are the graduates of the more orthodox and pietistic theological faculties.
Barth attributed this impasse to the two central emphases of
liberal theology. The first is its "religious individualism." It
seemed to Barth that liberalism's rejection of all norms of
revelation and authority external to the individual believer
led to a concentration upon the subjective and personal experience of the individual Christian. The second characteristic
of liberalism Barth designated as its emphasis upon "historical relativism." Because liberalism accepted the tenet of the
prevailing historiography that there were no absolutes in
history and therefore none in the realm of revelation or religion, it became necessary to treat the biblical witness to
revelation in the same manner as all other similar phenomena
in the history of religion. Barth summed up the outcome of
this approach as follows: "Religion knows only individual
values; history knows only general truths."[8]

When Barth wrote these words, he was a troubled devotee
of the theological liberalism in which he had been trained.
Later he depicted his stance in this period as follows:

> To the prevailing tendency of about 1910 among the younger
> followers of Albrecht Ritschl I attached myself with passable
> conviction. Yet it was not without a certain alienation in view
> of the issue of this school in the philosophy of Ernst Troeltsch,
> in which I found myself disappointed in regard to what inter-
> ested me in theology, although for the time being I did not see
> a better way before me.[9]

In 1911 Barth became the pastor of the Reformed Church
of Safenwil in north central Switzerland. He served as pastor
of this village church until 1921, and the theological revolution associated with his name came to birth in this small
industrial village surrounded by the scenic Swiss landscape.

Whoever would understand the genesis of Barth's theology must envisage him as a pastor faced with what he once described as "the need and promise of Christian preaching." The first years in Safenwil were not marked by any sharp break with his quasi-liberal theology. The most significant events of these years were his marriage to Nelly Hoffman (1913) and the renewal of his friendship with a former fellow student from Marburg, Eduard Thurneysen, now a neighboring pastor in Leutwil. These kindred spirits met frequently and carried on a lively correspondence about common concerns when personal visits were not possible.[10]

In an address to a group of ministers in 1922, Barth provides us with an important statement concerning the context in which his theological reorientation took place:

> For twelve years I was a minister, as all of you are. I *had* my theology. It was not really mine, to be sure, but that of my unforgotten teacher, Wilhelm Hermann [sic.], grafted upon the principles which I had learned, less consciously than unconsciously, in my native home—the principles of those Reformed Churches which today I represent and am honored to represent in an official capacity. Once in the ministry, I found myself growing away from those theological habits of thought and being forced back at every point more and more upon the specific *minister's* problem, the *sermon*. I sought to find my way between the problem of human life on the one hand and the content of the Bible on the other. As a minister I wanted to speak to the *people* in the infinite contradiction of their life, but to speak the no less infinite message of the *Bible*, which was as much of a riddle as life.[11]

Through the influence of Thurneysen, Barth was introduced to the eschatological theology of Johann Christoph Blumhardt (1805–1880). This Lutheran pietist pastor had founded a retreat center in the German village of Bad Boll after having experienced the healing of a deranged girl through the power of his prayers in her behalf. He interpreted this event as a sign of the inbreak of the kingdom of

God and of the victory of Christ over the forces of evil and
darkness. His son Christoph assumed the leadership of this
movement and stressed the manner in which commitment to
the kingdom of God necessitated concern for men in all
facets of their individual and social needs. Christoph Blumhardt provided a powerful impetus to the development of
the Swiss religious-socialist movement by his contacts with
Ragaz and Kutter, its two leaders. They criticized the prevailing conservatism of Swiss Protestantism which restricted
salvation to the individual soul, and called instead for a
recognition of the social dimension of the kingdom of God
and of its movement in history.

Both Thurneysen and Barth became Christian socialists.
Barth sided with the workers of Safenwil and of his congre-
gation in their struggle for a just wage. Later Thurneysen
wrote: "Socialism . . . was the movement that was to us the
most impressive parable, if not the substance, of the Kingdom
of God, which we preached on Sundays." [12] In 1915, Barth
joined the Social-Democratic Party—a thing quite unheard
of for a minister in that day. In a letter to Thurneysen dated
February 5, 1915, he states that this decision was prompted
because "it was no longer possible for me personally to remain suspended in the clouds above the present evil world
but rather it had to be demonstrated here and now that faith
in the Greatest does not exclude but rather includes within
it work and suffering in the realm of the imperfect." [13]

We have noted that Barth's theological reorientation was
a gradual one. It is erroneous to single out one event as the
cause of the new theological direction he was to pursue. The
Blumhardts and the religious-socialist movement each had
its effect. One must also recall that for Barth the prevailing
school of theological liberalism lost much of its luster when
ninety-three German intellectuals, including some of Barth's
former theological teachers, signed a manifesto in August,
1914, supporting the Kaiser and the German war policy.
Gradually but surely it became evident to Barth and Thurneysen that liberal theology had been weighed in the bal-

ances and found wanting. They gave themselves assiduously to the preparations of their sermons and serious biblical study, and published the first of several jointly authored sermon books in 1917 entitled *Suchet Gott, So Werdet Ihr Leben!* (Seek God and You Shall Live).

The clearest indication of Barth's changing position can be found in an address from 1916 entitled "The Strange New World Within the Bible." In it he enjoins his hearers to turn to the Bible in faith when in search for the Word of God for their day. "The Holy Scriptures will interpret themselves in spite of all our human limitations . . . . the Bible unfolds to us as we are met, guided, drawn on, and made to grow by the grace of God." [14] The real question with which Barth was wrestling in these days was that of the content of the Bible. He concedes that history, morality, and religion are all to be found in the Bible, but they do not represent its central interest. The answer concerning its content which Barth proposes remained characteristic of his later theological position:

> It is not the right human thoughts about God which form the content of the Bible, but the right divine thoughts about men. The Bible tells us not how we should talk with God but what he says to us; not how we find the way to him, but how he has sought and found the way to us; not the right relation in which we must place ourselves to him, but the covenant which he has made with all who are Abraham's spiritual children and which he has sealed once and for all in Jesus Christ. It is this which is within the Bible. The word of God is within the Bible. [15]

It was this Word within the words of the Bible which Barth sought to hear more clearly. Increasingly, he immersed himself in exegetical studies. Thurneysen informs us that in addition to the two published editions of his commentary on Romans, Barth completed unpublished studies of Ephesians and 2 Corinthians. It was, however, Barth's exposition of Romans which was destined to mark the dawn

of a new theological era. Beginning in 1916, Barth kept
extensive notes of his interpretation of that epistle which had
so often effected reformation in the history of the church.
By 1918, he had completed a lengthy commentary, but had
difficulty in finding a publisher. Finally, in 1919 a small
publisher in Bern printed 1,000 copies of the first edition of
Der Römerbrief. Barth tells us of his intention in this book
in the opening words of the preface to the first edition:

> Paul, as a child of his age, addressed his contemporaries. It
> is, however, far more important that, as Prophet and Apostle
> of the Kingdom of God, he veritably speaks to all men of
> every age. The differences between then and now, there and
> here, no doubt require careful investigation and consideration.
> But the purpose of such investigation can only be to demon-
> strate that these differences are, in fact, purely trivial.[16]

In this vein, Barth acknowledges the rightful place of
the modern historical-critical method of biblical interpretation. However, he affirms that the traditional Protestant doctrine of inspiration operated on a deeper level in seeking to
apprehend the true meaning of the text. Thus Barth broke
with the concentration on the philological and historical
study of the biblical text which characterized the commen-
taries of modern liberalism. His concern was "to see through
and beyond history into the spirit of the Bible, which is the
Eternal Spirit." [17]

A brief word concerning the first edition of Barth's commentary and its reception is in order. Clearly, this book
marks the beginning of Barth's break with the anthropocentric and cultural Christianity of theological liberalism.
His concern throughout is to magnify the sovereignty of God
rather than the religiosity of man. The Reformation emphasis upon man's radical fallenness is sounded with prophetic
power. However, at this stage Barth had not yet broken completely with the concept of man's capacity to see his oneness
with God once the divine kingdom has entered history. In
short, Barth was still under the influence of Platonic and

idealistic thought forms, and therefore could still speak more of continuity between God and man than he was subsequently able to do. Nevertheless, this book struck a responsive chord among many experiencing the bitter aftermath of the Great War. Though some acknowledged Barth's prophetic powers, others chided him for his disparagement of scientific exegesis. Yet others found his addiction to Kantian, Platonic, socialistic, and other categories reprehensible.

Barth learned from his critics where he could, but as was often to be the case, he remained his own severest critic. It was Barth's dissatisfaction with what he had said which led to the radically revised second edition in which as he wrote, "it may be claimed that no stone remains in its old place."[18] It was this second edition of Barth's commentary, published in 1922, which marked the rise of a new theological era associated with the name of Karl Barth. Confronted with the impact of this book, Karl Adam exclaimed that it "fell like a bomb on the playground of the theologians."

THE *EPISTLE TO THE ROMANS* (1922)

Three years intervened between the publication of the first and second editions of *Der Römerbrief* (1919–1922). After completing his revision in 1921, Barth accepted the call to become professor of Reformed Theology at the University of Göttingen, where he remained until 1925. How are we to account for the "change of front" which is evident in the second edition? Barth lists some of the factors accounting for it.

Most significant for Barth was a deeper involvement with Paul and the Roman epistle. Second, Franz Overbeck, the enigmatic church historian of Basel (1837–1905), a colleague and friend of Friedrich Nietzsche, had impressed Barth with his polemic against the prevailing form of cultural Christianity characteristic of liberal theology. Like a voice crying in the wilderness, Overbeck pointed repeatedly —to little avail—to the radically eschatological nature of

Christianity. Barth was among those who heeded his voice.
Third, through the influence of his brother Heinrich, Barth's
grasp of the thought of Plato and Kant became more sure.
Fourth, through Thurneysen, Barth had been introduced to
the Russian novelist Feodor Dostoevsky, from whom he
gained valuable insights into the predicament of man as
sinner. Fifth, there is the influence of the Dane, Kierkegaard
(1813–1855), whose theology of paradox had made little
impression on the course of German theology. It is generally
held that Barth is indebted to this Danish genius for the
dialectical method so characteristic of this second edition.
Barth's frequent references to "paradox," "decision," and
"crisis" in the attempt to describe the divine-human encounter are all reminiscent of Kierkegaard. What is more, we
must recall Barth's significant statement which reveals both
the guiding presupposition of his method of biblical exposition and his debt to Kierkegaard:

> ... if I have a system, it is limited to a recognition of what
> Kierkegaard called the 'infinite qualitative distinction' be-
> tween time and eternity, and to my regarding this as possess-
> ing negative as well as positive significance: 'God is in heaven,
> and thou art on earth.' The relation between such a God and
> such a man, and the relation between such a man and such a
> God, is for me the theme of the Bible and the essence of
> philosophy. Philosophers name this KRISIS of human percep-
> tion—the Prime Cause: the Bible beholds at the same cross-
> roads—the figure of Jesus Christ.[19]

A few other influences must be mentioned in conclusion.
Barth received some inspiration from Nietzsche's vision of
authentic Christianity which transcends its cultural and human expressions. Furthermore, it must be remembered that
since Barth's primary concern was the interpretation of Paul,
the guides he found helpful were important. Significantly,
Luther and Calvin receive special mention. Modern critical
scholars were utilized, but they were not as helpful in get-
ting to the heart of the text's meaning as the Reformers or

Johann Christian von Hofmann, J. T. Beck, and even Schlatter. All of the latter, like the Reformers, were concerned with the dialogue between the "original record" and the "reader" as they became involved with the text's "subject-matter, until a distinction between yesterday and to-day becomes impossible."[20]

A brief treatment of Barth's dialectical method and of some of the main themes of the *Römerbrief* must conclude our analysis of this creative period in Barth's theological pilgrimage. The use of dialectics is so prominent in this commentary that it gave rise to the designation of Barth's thought as "dialectical theology" or "crisis" theology. At one point, Barth traces the roots of the dialectical method to the Reformers and Paul.[21] In addition, Barth's adoption of the Kierkegaardian principle helps to account for the strongly dialectical character of his thought. In contrast, Barth's earlier thinking was less dialectical. There we find greater stress on the continuity between man and God, earth and heaven, immanence and transcendence. In this period, however, Barth needed some method by which to point to the "infinite qualitative distinction" between God and man, between time and eternity.

Several factors commended the method of dialectics. First, in it "there is an unwavering insight into the fact that the living truth, the determining content of any real utterance concerning God, is that God (but really God!) becomes man (but really man!)."[22] Second, the method of dialectics recognizes that all theology represents, figuratively speaking, a dialogue between God and man. Here there must be speech and response, "yes" and "no," question and answer. If there is to be real understanding in theology, this dialogue must be continuous. Hence the answer becomes the question again. This movement between question and answer, word and response, always involves two persons, God and man. Indeed, the ultimate source of all dialectical thinking for Barth is the God-man, Jesus Christ. Since this name involves both God and man, we are forbidden—if we are dialectical theolo-

gians—to regard this as one word. From this center, therefore, all thought proceeds dialectically. To be sure, man
searches for the single word which will overcome the para-
doxes inherent in this method. But whenever this is done, man
is guilty of overlooking the fact that all theologizing is frag-
mentary in nature. All theology, therefore, must be that of the
pilgrim (*theologia viatorum*). No human word can give expression to the divine truth in its entirety or purity. This is
reserved for God himself—who is the truth.

> He [God] speaks the one undialectical word. He utters the
> Amen which settles matters—which does not stand in need of
> further supplementation. He dissolves the disturbing "and."
> His theology, his knowledge and speaking about himself, is no
> *theologia viatorum*. It is undialectical theology. But we are
> men. That is the simplest and most decisive reason for the
> exclusive possibility of dialectical theology. It must, however,
> be true that the proper, the final, the decisive word be left to
> God.[23]

Barth's use of dialectics in this period led some critics to
interpret him quite mistakenly as a philosophical dialecti-
cian. We have seen, however, that his concern was theological. The dialectical method was the medium he adopted to
point to the message of the Word of God to man as he stands
in the situation of crisis between time and eternity. This crisis
was for Barth a sign of God's judgment upon all human
attempts to control and domesticate God and his revelation.
Above all, Barth was concerned to show that the "no" of
God's judgment fell particularly upon man's piety, religion,
philosophy, and morality—for all of them represented man's
attempts at self-salvation. Tillich is therefore right in remind-
ing us that "Barth's *Commentary on Romans* . . . was neither
a commentary nor a system, but a prophetic call addressed to
religion and culture, to acknowledge the divinity of the divine
and to dissolve the neo-Protestant synthesis between God's
and man's creativity." [24]

Some critics of the early Barth portrayed him as a pessimist whose message of doom and judgment was to be accounted for by the disillusionment following in the wake of the catastrophic events of World War I. Though the effect of the war upon Barth should not be minimized, it represented more the occasion for the development of certain of his insights rather than their cause. Nor is it correct to accuse the early Barth of accentuating man's predicament as sinner and the divine judgment to the total neglect of any mention of God's grace. He was, to be sure, concerned to counter all theologies which either denied God's transcendence or made it superfluous because of their concentration upon man and his goodness. But that is not to say that Barth pictured humanity as without hope. There is a possible resolution of man's crisis, but it can only come from God's side, from *jenseits*, from above and beyond man and his possibilities. In Jesus Christ, God, the Wholly Other, the Hidden One, breaks vertically into our history. But his coming is like a tangent touching a circle; Jesus Christ neither becomes identified with our history nor does he in any way come under man's control. He is the eschatological event signaling the beginning of the new world in his resurrection from the dead—an event which is *the* miracle effected by God. But he did come, and Barth could say, "Grace is the gift of Christ, who exposes the gulf which separates God and man, and, by exposing it, bridges it." [25] Or again, "The only way is the Way, and that Way is Christ." [26]

Thus we can say that Barth heard the divine "yes" sounding above the "no." Beyond and behind the divine wrath, there is God's mercy manifest in Jesus Christ. But how is he to be known? The answer is not directly, but through faith alone. But faith is not some latent capacity in man, as much of the theology of the nineteenth century held. It is not one human possibility among others. Humanly speaking, faith is something incredible. Whenever it exists, a miracle has taken place. Expressed differently, to have faith in Jesus as the Christ means for Barth to believe in his resurrection, and this is effected only through the work of the Holy Spirit. [27] Thus,

like Calvin, Barth accents anew the sovereignty of God and
the *sola gratia* of the Reformers. However, neither for Paul
nor for his interpreter Karl Barth did the note of judgment
override the major theme, namely, God's grace. Like Abra-
ham, men should fear God, but they should also hear the
divine "yes" within the divine "no." Had Barth not per-
ceived this truth, he could not have written as follows:

> Henceforward the negation in which we stand can be under-
> stood only in the light of the divine affirmation from which it
> proceeds. This means that the marks of human unrighteous-
> ness and ungodliness are crossed by the deeper marks of the
> divine forgiveness; that the discord of human defiance is
> penetrated by the undertones of the divine melody 'Neverthe-
> less.'[28]

This note of grace is also quite prominent in the sermons
of this period. At one place Barth writes:

> In God the Yes and No exist only for the sake of the Yes.
> People who have heard the divine "however" no longer won-
> der about the Yes and this No. They go about, they labor, they
> pray; as prisoners they carry about with them something of
> the freedom of the coming world. Alarmed, yet steadfast in
> spirit, they are already now God's witnesses and way-prepar-
> ers. Let no one say, "I cannot bear to hear this." Jesus has
> said words which also touch our lives. "I am the resurrection
> and the life."[29]

Thus Barth's dialectical theology intended to make clear
that the final word is always the divine word. Accordingly, a
proper theological method acknowledges the infinite qualitative difference between God and man; it recognizes that all
theology is theology of man, the sinner. In the last analysis,
therefore, even a dialectical theology can in no way guaran-
tee that it points Godward. This is beyond its power. Here it
is therefore apparent that all natural theology which proceeds
from man to God is ruled out. Man's knowledge of God is

always wholly dependent upon the divine prerogative and initiative. It was this emphasis which thundered and echoed throughout this commentary. In a sense, this is to wish to express the inexpressible, namely, that in Jesus Christ the hidden God (*Deus absconditus*) is the revealed God (*Deus revelatus*). Yet this is the theme of Paul's letter which cries out for expression.[30] Like Paul, the one thing that Man can do is to witness to that event. "The Moment when God, not man, speaks and acts, is the Moment of Miracle. And men have attained the utmost limit of their vigorous action when, possessing the status of John the Baptist, and filled with awe, they bear witness to God and to His Miracle."[31]

By the year 1922 and the publication of the second *Römerbrief*, Barth could trace his theological ancestry in a line running back through Kierkegaard to Luther and Calvin and finally to Paul and Jeremiah. Regarding Schleiermacher, the father of modern liberal theology, Barth wrote: "With all due respect to the genius shown in his work, I can *not* consider Schleiermacher a good teacher in the realm of theology because, so far as I can see, he is disastrously dim-sighted in regard to the fact that man as man is not only in *need* but beyond all hope of saving himself."[32]

As he reflected on his position in theology in 1922, Barth confessed that it did not seem to represent a position at all, "but rather a *mathematical* point upon which one cannot stand—a *view*point merely. With theology proper I have hardly made a start."[33] In the same vein he referred to his theology as "marginal note," a "corrective," a "pinch of spice" (Kierkegaard). The tentativeness with which Barth held to the dialectical method may be seen in the closing words of an address in 1922. He asks: "Can theology, should theology, pass beyond *prolegomena* to Christology? It may be that everything is said in the prolegomena."[34]

Barth's newly assumed duties as a professor of theology at Göttingen, along with reflection upon the service his theology had performed in calling the liberal interpretation of the gospel into question, made it increasingly apparent that he

must give attention to the task of positive, theological con-
struction. Later he could say: "Theology could and ought
not to be a 'theology of crisis' for longer than a moment."[35]
We will give attention to these changes in the ensuing pages.
We may anticipate by saying that Barth's concern was the
positive development of a theology of the Word of God.
Eventually, this was to mean a radically christocentric theology. In 1922, however, Barth had not yet envisaged what
form a radically christocentric theology would take. When in
that same year Barth, Gogarten, Thurneysen, and Georg
Merz joined together to establish the periodical *Zwischen den
Zeiten* (Between the Times), the cohesive factor in their fellowship was a common desire to provide a medium for the
expression of a biblical theology of the Word of God which
would be opposed to the neo-Protestant or liberal version of
the gospel. At first, Bultmann, Brunner, and others identified
with this new direction, even though sharp differences between Barth and Bultmann soon became evident. The journal
exercised considerable influence upon the course of German
theology until it was discontinued in 1933, the year of
Hitler's rise to power. By that time someone could remark
that the leaders of the dialectical theology were in as much
disagreement as the "generals of the Chinese revolution."[36]

TRANSITION TO DOGMATICS, 1922–1932

Barth's transition from a Swiss village pastor to a theological
professor filled him with many misgivings. A letter from his
friend Thurneysen, written shortly after Barth's arrival in
Göttingen, seems to capture their common feeling that less
demanding days were a thing of the past. "Now Safenwil has
been left behind and in place of it there is a very great re-
moteness, a strangeness, a mystery, a loneliness, a wasteland,
sea, wind, waves."[37] In many ways Barth felt ill-equipped to
fulfill the responsibilities expected of him. His letters to
Thurneysen dating from the early years in Göttingen reveal

the anxiety which the daily pressure to lecture occasioned in the fledgling professor. On one occasion he wrote:

> Recently it happened to me that at three o'clock in the morning I recognized that what I had written on *De foedere* (Concerning the Covenant) for the next morning was nonsense and dangerously false teaching. I had simply to cancel the lecture at eight o'clock.[38]

In spite of these difficulties, Barth worked assiduously on his lectures on the Reformed tradition. The Heidelberg Catechism, Calvin, Zwingli, and Schleiermacher were the subjects of successive courses. His letters also indicate that Barth was immersed in an intensive study of the whole history of theology and especially the theology of the Reformers. This disciplined study was to stand him in good stead. Yet in 1924 when Barth felt it necessary to begin lecturing in dogmatics or systematic theology, he was not certain of the direction to take. Later he wrote of his feelings at that time: "No one can ever have been more plagued than I was with the problem, could I do it? and how?"[39] In the face of this impasse, Barth came across a new edition of Heinrich Heppe's *Reformed Dogmatics*, a compilation of seventeenth-century Protestant orthodox theology. Though Barth had assumed a negative attitude toward orthodoxy in his earlier days, he writes of his discovery:

> I read, I studied, I reflected; and found that I was rewarded with the discovery that here at last I was in the atmosphere in which the road, by way of the Reformers to Holy Scriptures, was a more sensible and natural one to tread than the atmosphere, now only too familiar to me, of the theological literature determined by Schleiermacher and Ritschl. I found a dogmatics which had both form and substance, oriented upon the central indication of the Biblical evidences for revelation, which it also managed to follow out in detail with astonishing richness.[40]

Barth's entry into the circle of German theology was not
without its difficulties. When he proposed to offer a course in
dogmatics in 1924, he was opposed by his Lutheran colleagues on the theological faculty at Göttingen who wanted
only Lutheran dogmatics taught! They insisted that Barth
should designate his course "Reformed Dogmatics" in keeping with his chair and title. Never one to retreat, Barth entitled his lectures—following Calvin—"Instruction in the
Christian Religion." [41]

In spite of the difficulties of these years, Barth was becoming more and more a name to be reckoned with in German
theological circles. He gave numerous addresses, and in 1924
three of his books were published. In all of his writing and
lecturing, Barth struggled both to sharpen his critique of liberal theology and to construct a theology of the Word of God
which would aid the church's proclamation and understanding of the gospel.

In 1925 Barth accepted the invitation to become professor
of Dogmatics and New Testament Exegesis at the University
of Münster in Westphalia where he remained until 1930. Of
his four books published during this period, we must note a
collection of essays and addresses from the period 1920–28
entitled *Theology and Church* (1928; English translation,
1962). Even more significant was the publication in 1927 of
the fruit of Barth's initial labors in dogmatics—*Die christliche Dogmatik im Entwurf* (Christian Dogmatics in Outline). This initial volume, which was never translated into
English, was entitled *The Doctrine of the Word of God:
Prolegomena to Christian Dogmatics*. The book is of historical significance because it shows us the early shape of
Barth's systematic theological thinking. Although he acknowledges in the preface that he found some kindred spirits in
modern theology (I. A. Dorner, Kierkegaard, Julius Müller,
the Blumhardts, Hermann Friedrich Kohlbrügge, Hermann
Kutter, and A. F. C. Vilmar), there was no school of thought
which he could affirm. Even the position of his revered teacher, Wilhelm Herrmann, was regarded by Barth as the last stage

of a development which had to be abandoned. Thus it was
that Barth quite consciously adopted a position, as he did in
the *Römerbrief,* which marked a radical departure from the
course of Protestant theology during the preceding two
centuries.[42]

Barth's historical proximity to theological liberalism made
it imperative that his polemic against it be clear and cogent.
He remarked that it was all too easy to feel more at home in
the theological climate of neo-Protestantism than in the heri-
tage of the Reformers. Increasingly, however, Barth saw
nothing promising in the continuation of liberalism. His attitude is put sharply in an address of 1928:

> If I today became convinced that the interpretation of the
> Reformation on the line taken by Schleiermacher-Ritschl-
> Troeltsch (or even by Seeberg or Holl) was correct; that
> Luther and Calvin really intended such an outcome of their
> labours; I could not indeed become a Catholic tomorrow, but
> I should have to withdraw from the evangelical Church. And
> if I were forced to make a choice between the two evils, I
> should, in fact, prefer the Catholic.[43]

Christian Dogmatics in Outline (1927)

Where does Barth take his stand in his first attempt to
write a prolegomena to dogmatics? It is clear that he intends
to base his theology upon a position opposed both to Roman
Catholic theology which allows for a natural theology and to
the theology of the religious self-consciousness characteristic
of Protestant liberalism following Schleiermacher. What is
more, he rejects allowing any metaphysic or philosophy to
dictate the theologian's starting point or method. Therefore,
he intends to develop a theology grounded upon the Word of
God. Indeed, the entire prolegomena is conceived as an exposition of the doctrine of the Word of God. In contrast to
liberalism's concern with the Christian self-consciousness,
Barth's concern is with the Word of God addressed to man.

In this book, Barth is already discussing the Word of God

in its threefold form: the proclaimed Word, the written Word, and the revealed Word.[44] In every instance, the Word of God is to be understood as the speech of God, or the act of God, in which God is always the subject. Since God is the Lord of his Word, it never becomes the possession of man in the way in which neo-Protestants were eager to affirm.

Barth regards his starting with the Word of God as a radical departure from the liberal tradition in which he was schooled. There theology began with the investigation of the Christian's piety. Because for Barth, theology must begin with the Word of God, the proper subject of theology is this Word and not the faith of the believer, as Barth had once held. The Word of God is not, as liberalism maintained, contained in the faith of the believer, but faith is grounded and upheld by the Word of God. This does not mean that Barth denied the correlation between the Word of God and faith. Rather, he proposes to reestablish and preserve this correlation by accentuating the priority of God and his Word over man's faith.[45]

From this vantage point the main lines of Barth's mature doctrine of revelation are apparent. Jesus Christ, the revealed Word of God, is already understood as the objective possibility of revelation. To apprehend this Word necessitates the work of the Holy Spirit, the subjective possibility of revelation. But here, just as noted earlier, Barth will allow no fusion of the finite and the infinite: even in the faith moment, God remains God and man remains man.

It is significant that at this date Barth already interprets God in his revelation in terms of the doctrine of the Trinity. According to the testimony of Holy Scripture, the God who reveals himself is triune. Therefore Barth finds the classical doctrine of the Trinity to be the chief and necessary bulwark against every anthropocentric and natural theology. Whoever would affirm a natural theology must show that it has reference to the triune God who makes himself known in his revelation.[46]

At the point of man's reception of the Word of God, Barth

is somewhat ambiguous in this volume. His major concern seems to have been to teach that God, the Holy Spirit, makes it possible for man to hear and respond to the Word of God which is proclaimed or written. When Barth is engaged in a phenomenological analysis of the Word of God, this is the stress. However, Barth opted for the existential method when speaking about man's hearing the Word preached. This led him to say:

> The Word of God is not only speech, but address. We can never hurry hither or yon, neither into heaven nor into the abyss, in order to perceive or to read it, but it is come to us. That means: the hearing man is as much included within the concept of the Word of God as the speaking God. He is "co-posited" [*mitgesetzt*] with the Word in much the same manner as Schleiermacher's God is co-posited in the feeling of absolute dependence.[47]

In time it became apparent to Barth that the existential methodology which dominated his prolegomena prevented the Word of God from being rightly comprehended as it stands over against man. This accounts for the statement in the revised prolegomena of 1932 that it was necessary to "cut out in this second issue of the book everything that in the first issue might give the slightest appearance of giving to theology a basis, support, or even a mere justification in the way of existential philosophy."[48] To have continued along this line would have meant to capitulate to the anthropocentric theology which he sought to combat.

The Relation of Theology to Philosophy

It may be instructive at this juncture to pursue the manner in which Barth conceived of the relationship of theology to philosophy in 1927. He is quite aware that no one comes to the task of exegesis or theology without some presuppositions concerning the relationships between God, the world, and man. "In no case does anyone have the right . . . to pride himself . . . as though he were completely rid of the Greek influ-

ence, as though he did not confuse his Weltanschauung with
the New Testament, but rather allowed the text alone to speak
for itself."[49] The point at issue for Barth is not whether a
theologian utilizes philosophy in theologizing, but rather the
manner in which philosophy is used. That is, a particular
philosophy becomes a danger when the theologian is no longer
aware that it affects the manner in which he interprets the
gospel. Liberalism, for example, went astray because it was
no longer conscious of the extent to which its commitments to
philosophical rationalism or idealism influenced its interpretations of the Scriptures.

Conscious, therefore, of the dangers in this area, Barth
attempts to adopt an approach in exegesis which will mini-
mize the dangers implicit in a rigid adherence to a particular
metaphysic or *Weltanschauung*. This involves the adoption
of the biblical thought form (*Denkform*) or perspective. This
attitude is "the mind-set of the prophets and apostles. It is
not the attitude of observers . . . nor of philosophers, but that
of witnesses, of people who, whatever else they may be, speak
as those who are grounded in the reality of the 'and God
spake' as an absolute presupposition."[50] The controlling
factor in all of their thinking and speaking is the Word of
God (*Deus dixit*). It is this perspective which Barth regards
as the proper paradigm for both Christian preaching and
dogmatics. If the Word dominates, then philosophical and
other elements utilized by the theologian will be subordinated
to their rightful center. The theologian who starts with the
Word of God heard in faith minimizes the perils attending
theological efforts which begin with experience or history and
hope to conclude by speaking about God. In its essence, therefore, the biblical attitude is the antithesis of the apologetic
approach which presumes that somehow God may be known
without beginning with God.[51]

It is Barth's conviction that this mode of thinking may be
learned through the constant application of oneself to the
task of interpreting Holy Scripture. That is, one will begin
to think and speak in a confessional manner. Only in this way
can dogmatics be faithful to the Word of God. Here it should

be recalled that Barth's later references in the *Church Dogmatics* to the relationship of theology to philosophy do not differ from the position set forth in 1927. A few years later Barth summed up his conception of the theologian's attitude toward philosophy nicely in these words: "All things are lawful for me, but nothing [save the Word of God] shall take me captive."[52]

Anselm: Faith in Search of Understanding (1931)

The second publication of this crucial decade in Barth's development which demands attention is perhaps Barth's least read book. In 1930, Barth left Münster to become professor of systematic theology at the University of Bonn. There he continued his practice of offering seminars on the history of theology. One of the first seminars dealt with Anselm's *Cur Deus Homo*. This precipitated further study of Anselm and his theological method. In 1931, these labors bore fruit in Barth's book on Anselm's proof for the existence of God within the context of his theological program entitled *Fides quaerens intellectum* (Faith in Search of Understanding).

In one of his revealing autobiographical statements concerning how he "changed his mind" from 1928–1938, Barth refers to the significance of this book for his theology.

> The *deepening* [of my theological position] consisted in this: in these years I have had to rid myself of the last remnants of a philosophical, i.e., anthropological (in America one says "humanistic" or "naturalistic") foundation and exposition of Christian doctrine. The real document of this farewell is, in truth, not the much-read . . . *Nein!*, directed against Brunner in 1934, but rather the book about the evidence for God of Anselm of Canterbury which appeared in 1931. Among all my books I regard this as the one written with the greatest satisfaction. And yet in America it is doubtless not read at all and in Europe it certainly is the least read of any of my works.[53]

Why did Barth hold Anselm in such high regard? In the preface Barth states that he considers Anselm's proof for the existence of God to be a perceptive and sound piece of theology, which, if heeded, could be instructive both for modern Protestant and Catholic theology in terms of what constitutes an adequate theological method. It is noteworthy that at the outset of the important section in the *Church Dogmatics* dealing with the knowledge of God Barth wrote: ". . . I learned the fundamental attitude to the problem of the knowledge and existence of God . . . at the feet of Anselm."[54] Put more generally we can say that Anselm helped Barth develop the theological method characteristic of the entire *Church Dogmatics*. In short, Anselm taught Barth how theology should be done.

Barth's concern in his analysis of Anselm's theological method is evident in the title of his study, *Fides quaerens intellectum*, which is the original title of Anselm's *Proslogion*. This Anselmic phrase is a variation of Augustine's dictum that "unless you believe, you will not understand." The crucial problem for theological method here is: what is the relationship between faith and knowledge, or why does faith seek "understanding"? Or we could put it a bit differently and ask: How do we move from the moment of faith to theology? Barth holds that a polemic and apologetic intention does motivate Anselm's desire for understanding. But neither this nor the joy which accompanies the clarification of one's faith through reason provides the primary motivation for this quest. Barth follows Anselm in holding that faith seeks understanding because this movement is characteristic of the nature of faith as such. Barth summarizes this drive of faith for deepened understanding and more certain knowledge of God, its object, as follows: *"Credo ut intelligam* [I believe in order that I might understand] means: It is my very faith itself that summons me to knowledge."[55]

Barth reminds us that in order to comprehend how the program of "faith seeking understanding" is carried out, we must understand Anselm's concept of faith. Faith is not to be confused with something irrational or illogical. Barth paraphrases Anselm's understanding of faith as follows:

> Faith is the right act of the will if it is that which is owed to God and demanded by God, and bound together with a saving "experience"; that is, in so far as it is faith in *God,* in so far as it believes that which is *true.* Faith comes from hearing, and hearing comes from preaching. Faith is related to the "Word of Christ" and it is not faith if it is not the reception, that is, knowledge and acknowledgement of the "Word of Christ." [56]

For Barth and Anselm, therefore, we do not begin our quest for knowledge of God apart from faith. Rather, we must begin with faith in the Word of Christ or the Word of God which has been spoken. The Scriptures and ancient church Confessions are the highest expressions of the church's *Credo* or faith. The individual Christian's faith (*credo*) must hold to the understanding of Christ in these norms if it is to be true faith.

Barth sees the progression from faith to understanding in Anselm something like this. First, at the initial level of faith there is a certain knowledge or understanding concerning the words which proclaim Christ. This is an intellectual comprehension which even the unbeliever may share. But in the second place, faith moves beyond this logical understanding of the truth affirmed to an understanding of the reality behind the words. Thus in faith, Christ who is proclaimed is acknowledged. Faith, then, stands both at the beginning and the end of the quest for understanding: we move from faith to faith. Expressed otherwise, the quest for understanding on the part of the believer moves from faith toward sight—an apprehension which will be fully realized only in the *eschaton.*[57]

Barth contends that it is precisely because the beginning and end of the process of understanding are present in faith that theology is possible. The success or failure of faith's attempt to reach more complete understanding in no way threatens its existence. For theology exists neither to lead one to faith nor to free from doubt. Nor does it try to storm the heavens or require a sacrifice of one's intellect. The theologian can do his task in the recognition that all human knowledge of God, including that contained within the Confession (*Credo*) of the church, is dependent for its validation upon the revelation of God.[58]

In this connection it is important to note that Barth, like Anselm, stresses that theology must be carried on in faith from within the circle of faith, the church. The theologian proceeds within these limits, affirming the "thatness" of the revelation affirmed in the church's *Credo* or Confession. Throughout the *Church Dogmatics*, Barth reiterates that the theologian must presuppose that God has acted and revealed himself. The process of seeking understanding in which he engages—though never complete—can and does issue in the true knowledge of God. Man's statements and language about God may become analogous to their object; they may be true theological statements.

In adopting this position, Barth has moved beyond some of the radical statements of his period of dialectical theology where the incongruity between God and man was so great that it appeared that man's language could never point to God. Balthasar, an astute Roman Catholic interpreter of Barth, is therefore correct in identifying a major shift in Barth's thinking as the movement from a theology of dialectics to a theology based on analogy. That is to say, man's knowledge of God becomes conformable to its object (God) through faith and through the divine grace. Because this event and process takes place—as both Anselm and Barth affirm— "faith can seek understanding" and theology can be the most beautiful of sciences![59]

It should be clear from the foregoing why Barth rejects the widespread interpretation of Anselm as a rationalist who moves from the question of the possibility of revelation to its necessity or reality on the basis of rational argumentation and proofs. It is Barth's contention that Anselm always began in faith or with the Confession of the church (the reality of revelation) and then proceeded to ask which kind of theological reflection and argumentation was appropriate to the subject under consideration.[60] He cannot therefore be regarded as a kind of "patron saint" of natural theology or even as an apologetic theologian in the modern sense of that term. Barth's final argument against treating Anselm as a rationalist is found in the intimate relationship he posits between theology and prayer. It is not enough to say that for Anselm there is no true knowledge of God apart from God's prevenient and continuing grace. The attainment of true knowledge of God lies beyond the powers of human reason and must be prayed for constantly. Moreover, were it not for the fact that God made himself known to man once and again and again through his grace, faith could never comprehend God. Barth adopts and underscores this position in the *Church Dogmatics* by referring to "prayer as the attitude apart from which dogmatic work is impossible."[61]

In the next chapter the extent to which Barth adopts Anselm's theological method will become more apparent. However, we may make several generalizations at this point. First, it is evident that for Barth faith is dependent for its existence upon the event of revelation. Second, only where faith in God's revelation exists can we speak about true knowledge of God. Third, the fuller knowledge which issues from faith's continuing quest for understanding may be true knowledge of God.

Regin Prenter is of the opinion that Barth's methodology is in agreement with Anselm's to the extent that he acknowledges the testimony of Holy Scripture to the revelation in Jesus Christ as the unifying center from which all of the relationships in this revelation must be explained. The consistency with which Barth interprets all doctrines quite logically from that point is, in Prenter's opinion, probably without parallel in the history of theology. Prenter observes:

> The rigorous consistency which Barth seeks in the course of understanding the theology of revelation imparts a completeness and logic to his theological thinking which makes him one of the greatest thinkers in all of Christendom. His *Church Dogmatics* is, therefore, also a true theological system, perhaps the greatest in all of history.[62]

THE PERIOD OF THE *CHURCH DOGMATICS*,
1932–1968

Since the remaining chapters will deal with the theology of
the *Church Dogmatics*, the conclusion of this chapter is
restricted to a brief account of important events in Barth's
life. The decade of the thirties was an eventful one for
Barth. Because of his dissatisfaction with his first attempt at
dogmatics in *Christian Dogmatics in Outline* (1927), he revised this introduction and it was published in 1932 with the
title *The Doctrine of the Word of God*. The revision was the
first half-volume of Barth's *Church Dogmatics* (K.D. I/1).
With its appearance it became evident that the ranks of the
dialectical theology were dissolving. Barth's starting point
in the Word of God led him to break with Bultmann and Gogarten, whose approach seemed too reminiscent of liberalism.

The decisive event in the thirties which influenced the
course of Barth's life was Hitler's installation as Chancellor
of Germany early in 1933. In July of 1933, Barth and Thurneysen established a theological journal entitled *Theologische
Existenz heute* (Theological Existence Today). In its pages
Barth and like-minded colleagues voiced their vehement
opposition to Hitler and the "German Christians." The latter
advocated a synthesis of German National Socialism and the
gospel, and were recognized as the official Church of Germany
by Hitler. Barth's prophetic call for the Christian church in
Germany to acknowledge none but Jesus Christ as her *Führer*
did not go unheeded. He became the leading theological spokes-
man of the Confessing Church which opposed the German
Christians and Hitler. He and others in this minority movement refused to identify the gospel with the Nazi concerns for
"Nation, Race and *Führer*." The Confessing Church met at
Barmen, Germany, in 1934 and declared its faith in what is
known as the Barmen Confession. While some took their
afternoon naps, Barth wrote the draft which later was accepted and disseminated as the Barmen Confession. Its pro-

phetic first article calls for obedience to Jesus Christ alone "in life and in death." [63] It is noteworthy that theology, church, and action were inextricably interrelated in these significant years in Barth's theological pilgrimage.

Barth's breach in 1934 with his former colleague, Emil Brunner, over the question of natural theology was so sharp because Barth felt that any form of natural theology would lend support to the German Christian cause and detract from the supremacy of the revelation of God in Jesus Christ. Though Barth and Brunner later lived for years in close physical proximity as they taught in Basel and Zurich respectively, not until the year 1960 was this friendship of earlier years restored through a friendly personal reunion.

Increasingly Barth became *persona non grata* in the eyes of the Nazi officials. He refused to begin his classes in Bonn with the customary *Heil Hitler!*—and he would not swear unconditional allegiance to the *Führer*. As a result, he was dismissed from his teaching post and expelled from Germany. He was called immediately to become the professor of theology at the University of Basel where he began teaching in 1935 at the age of forty-nine. From this vantage point just across the Rhine from Germany, Barth kept in close touch with both church and political struggles in Germany. In these years, he took advantage of the opportunity for travel in Europe, visiting Italy and then Hungary in 1936–37. During 1937–38, he visited Scotland to deliver the Gifford Lectures. Above all else, he concentrated on the *Church Dogmatics*. Two more volumes were completed during the thirties. The final volume of the prolegomena (K.D. I/2), developed as an exposition of *The Doctrine of the Word of God*, appeared in 1938 (C.D. I/2, 1956). The first volume of *The Doctrine of God* (K.D. II/1) appeared in 1940 (C.D. II/1, 1957). During the late thirties and in the early forties after the outbreak of World War II, Barth wrote letters to Czechs, French Protestants, and to the English, Norwegians, Dutch, and Americans threatened by the Nazis, urging them to resist Naziism.

During the war Barth was also required to serve in the Swiss army. So at the age of fifty-four, he helped guard the Swiss border at Basel from German intruders!

When Barth fled to Basel in 1935, he thought that he would resettle in Germany when conditions permitted. However, this was not to be. He did return briefly to Germany in 1945 and several times thereafter. In the midst of the chaos and hardship occasioned by Germany's bitter defeat, Barth angered the Swiss as well as Germany's victors by encouraging them to grant the German people "political freedom" as soon as possible. Once again, Barth found it necessary to go against the stream of popular opinion as he hoped for a new day for the church in Germany and for the German people.

Barth's travels in the forties were intentionally restricted while he concentrated on the demands of writing the *Church Dogmatics*, which formed the basis of his lectures at Basel. During the years 1946 and 1947, Barth lectured to the decimated ranks of the German postwar theological generation as guest professor in his former post at Bonn. These lectures first appeared in English under the title *Dogmatics in Outline* (1949). In 1948, Barth visited Hungary and talked with leaders of the Reformed Church living under Communism. Upon his return to Basel, he wrote several open letters urging Christians in Hungary that it would be better "to evangelize the strayed and bewildered Hungarian people" than to "protest . . . against the obvious danger . . . in the Communist system."[64] For this stand Barth was accused of being "soft" on Communism, especially by certain American theologians. Barth's concern in the East-West struggle was to do all possible to lessen rather than to heighten hostilities and tensions. Recent events appear to have shown the wisdom of his decision in this regard. In 1948, Barth also took part in the meeting constituting the World Council of Churches in Amsterdam. Though he went with some misgivings, he noted later that he found this ecumenical endeavor stimulating and rewarding at most points.

The decade of the forties was significant for Barth's theological maturation and production. With the decision to remain in Basel behind him, Barth worked steadily on the *Church Dogmatics*. The publication of the doctrine of *The Election of God* (K.D. II/2) in 1942 shows a significant intensification of Barth's christological concentration (C.D. II/2, 1957). From this point on in the development of his dogmatics, there is a greater dynamic and movement than we find in the earlier volumes. This christological emphasis is quite evident in the other volumes of the dogmatics published in this decade and the early fifties. The *Doctrine of Creation* (K.D. III/1) appeared in 1945 (C.D. III/1, 1958). The second part of the third volume (K.D. III/2), dealing with the doctrine of man, followed in 1948 (C.D. III/2, 1960). At the beginning of a new decade, Barth's treatment of the doctrine of providence and of evil (K.D. III/3, 1950) was published (C.D. III/3, 1961).

In 1951 Barth completed the doctrine of creation in a volume dealing with ethics (K.D. III/4), specifically, the command of God the Creator, and the response of man in terms of his God-given freedom (C.D. III/4, 1961). Barth became sixty-five during this year and willingly accepted being referred to increasingly as "the old man in Basel."[65] However, his work as teacher, writer—and occasional lecturer elsewhere—continued unabated. Even though the years were taking their toll, Barth worked assiduously in the decade of the fifties on the doctrine of reconciliation. The three major volumes in Barth's massive reinterpretation of this doctrine appeared before the end of the decade. These were the following: K.D. IV/1 (1953, C.D. 1956); K.D. IV/2 (1955, C.D. 1958); K.D. IV/3-I (1959, C.D. 1961); and K.D. IV/3-II (1959, C.D. 1962).

Although Barth sharply curtailed his travel and lecturing beyond Basel during this decade, he preached with some frequency to inmates in the Basel prison—which he referred to as "my favorite pulpit."[66] The demands in Basel were great enough. Students from all parts of the world flocked to hear him in increasing numbers. To accommodate them, Barth provided colloquia in French and English in addition to his regular lectures in dogmatics and seminars. It was an unforgettable experience for this writer to be able to spend a year of postgraduate study in Basel during the academic year 1959–60. Along with many other foreigners, I found Professor Barth to be all that I had anticipated from his writings and from stories circulated about his wisdom, graciousness, and good humor. In short, he was an attractive human being.

In May of 1956, Barth celebrated his seventieth birthday. Though grateful for all of the remembrances he received, he was especially gratified to be asked by his fellow citizens in Basel to deliver the "memorial address" in connection with the celebration of the 200th anniversary of Mozart's birth. Long an admirer of Mozart, Barth said of him in reflecting on this occasion and on his music:

> I am not especially gifted or cultured artistically and certainly not inclined to confuse or identify the history of salvation with any part of the history of art. But the golden sounds and melodies of Mozart's music have from early times spoken to me not as gospel but as parables of the realm of God's free grace as revealed in the gospel—and they do so again and again with great spontaneity and directness. Without such music I could not think of that which concerns me personally in both theology and politics. . . . There are probably very few theological study rooms in which pictures of Calvin and Mozart are to be seen hanging next to each other and at the same height.[67]

The beginning of the final decade in Barth's life found him teaching as usual. However, instead of continuing to lecture on the ethics related to the doctrine of reconciliation in the winter semester of 1961–62 before his formal retirement in March, 1962, Barth delivered a series of lectures intended to "render a short account to myself and my contemporaries of what, up to now, I have basically sought, learned, and represented from among all the paths and detours in the field of evangelical theology. . . ."[68] After completing this series, he gave his final lecture at the University of Basel on March 1, 1962. The chosen theme—so central to his mature theology and the doctrine of reconciliation on which he had labored during the last decade—was the divine *agape* seeking man in Jesus Christ.

In April and May of 1962, Barth delivered the first five lectures of the above series to overflow audiences at the University of Chicago and at Princeton Theological Seminary. These and his final lectures at Basel were published with the title, *Evangelical Theology: An Introduction.* At the conclusion of an evening panel discussion between Barth and a panel of American theologians in the Rockefeller Memorial Chapel at the University of Chicago, the openness and dynamic of the tired but unbowed warrior was once more in evidence as he urged American theologians to develop a theology of freedom on the basis of the freedom granted the Christian through Christ. In the foreword to the American edition of *Evangelical Theology* he recalls his concluding remark in this vein:

> What we need on this and the other side of the Atlantic is not Thomism, Lutheranism, Calvinism, orthodoxy, religionism, existentialism, nor is it a return to Harnack and Troeltsch (and least of all is it "Barthianism"!), but what I somewhat cryptically called in my little final speech at Chicago a "theology of freedom" that looks ahead and strives forward. More or less or something other than that would scarcely be suitable, either here or there, to the foundation, object, and content of evangelical theology or to the nearly apocalyptic seriousness of our time.[69]

At the end of his first and last visit to the United States, Barth summed up his impressions with the word—"fantastic."[70] In his last years Barth was the recipient of numerous honorary degrees and prizes. His academic pursuits were interrupted by an extended illness lasting from the time of his return from America to Basel in 1962 until the fall of 1965. Yet he was able to celebrate his eightieth birthday in

May of 1966 in better health. He even traveled to Rome to
discuss and assess the results of the Second Vatican Council.
However, he remarked that the "later Barth" could neither
complete the *Church Dogmatics* nor even the projected volume on ethics in relationship to the doctrine of reconciliation.

In reply to many inquiries directed to him since 1960
concerning the completion of the *Church Dogmatics*, and particularly the projected volume on eschatology (K.D. V), Barth
took some delight in asking whether they had read what he
had said already on eschatology or whether they had finished
reading the *Church Dogmatics!* [71] After some hesitation he
allowed the publication of a final fragment introducing the
ethics related to the doctrine of reconciliation with the title
Baptism as the Foundation of the Christian Life (K.D. IV/4,
1967; C.D. 1969). Some words from the final preface Barth
was to write explain some reasons for its publication and
reveal him to be one who was not afraid to go "against the
stream" even as he neared the end of his earthly pilgrimage.

> ... today there is much ready talk (too much and too ready)
> about the world which is supposed to have come of age in
> relation to God. However that may be, my own concern is
> rather with the man who ought to come of age in relation to
> God and the world, i.e., the mature Christian and mature
> Christianity, its thought, speech and action in responsibility
> to God, in living hope in Him, in service to the world, in free
> confession and unceasing prayer. [72]

A little over a year and a half after Barth wrote these
words, "God took him home to his rest in the early hours of
December 10, 1968, the great Church Father of Evangelical Christendom, the one genuine Doctor of the Evangelical
Church the modern era has known." [73]

II. The Doctrine of Revelation and the Knowledge of God

INTRODUCTION: CHRISTOCENTRIC VS. ANTHROPOCENTRIC THEOLOGY

In the previous chapter we traced the main lines of Barth's theological development up to the year 1932. That year marks a watershed because in its course the revised first volume of Barth's prolegomena to his *Dogmatics* was published with the title *The Doctrine of the Word of God*. It is not without significance that Barth changed the general title of the entire series from *Christian Dogmatics* (1927) to *Church Dogmatics*, therewith indicating that theology is the church's reflection upon, and interpretation of, the revelation of God culminating in Jesus Christ.[1] During the next thirty years, Barth gave himself with unflagging zeal to writing his multivolumed *Dogmatics*. The last part-volume was published in 1967, some five years after Barth's official retirement as professor of Theology at the University of Basel (1935–62).

The reader approaching Barth's *Dogmatics* for the first time is understandably overwhelmed by its sheer massiveness. However, even the novice can understand the direction of Barth's theology in any single doctrine if he recalls that Barth intends first and last to be a theologian obedient to the Word of God. This means that sound theology is that which again and again fixes attention upon the God of the old and new covenants whose Word finds fulfillment in Jesus Christ.

Whenever, therefore, a theologian or denomination makes
something other than the revelation of God attested in Scripture normative, they have departed from the foundation
which provides the only secure basis for all theological
formulations.

If one looks at the *Church Dogmatics* in its entirety, one
must say that the decisive mark of Barth's theology is its
christocentricity. At the very outset of the prolegomena, Barth
affirms that the task of dogmatic theology is to discover the
extent to which the church's language about God points
toward the decisive revelation of God in Jesus Christ, who is
both the "essence of the Church" and the norm and measure
of her theology.[2] Since Jesus Christ himself is the way, the
truth and the life (John 14:6), theology's overriding concern
must be to witness faithfully to his significance for understanding all of the relationships between God and man and
between man and his fellowman.

In maintaining that Barth's christological method is the key
to interpreting his theology, we must keep in mind that Barth
himself did not envisage immediately the full implications of
this starting point. In the course of the *Church Dogmatics*,
the christological starting point and norm of his theology
became more and more prominent. He consciously goes beyond the Reformers in regarding Jesus Christ as the final
criterion of every theological statement. One may perhaps
single out Barth's doctrine of election (C.D. II/2), published
in 1942, as the clearest indication of the intensification of the
christocentric thrust of his theology. A key text for understanding both Barth's christocentric doctrine of election and
the whole of his theology is Colossians 1:19: "For in him all
the fullness of God was pleased to dwell. . ."[3] (RSV).

At this point, we cannot pursue the implications of Barth's
christocentricity for the whole of his theology. However, the
inclusion of several programmatic statements indicating the
significance Barth attaches to this approach may be helpful.
Thus, in the doctrine of reconciliation, he can say: "Jesus
Christ in His self-revelation is, therefore, the basic text . . ."

of all theology.[4] Somewhat earlier he spoke in a similar vein: "If it [Jesus Christ] were a principle and not a name indicating a person, we should describe it as the epistemological principle of the message."[5] These statements underlining Barth's christocentricity were anticipated in the doctrine of revelation, which is expounded in terms of Jesus Christ who is both the objective reality and possibility of revelation (C.D. I/2).

In attempting to develop a theology of the Word of God or a christocentric theology, Barth consciously sought to dissociate himself from what he regarded to be the heretical interpretations of revelation set forth in Protestant liberalism and Roman Catholicism. Let us look first a bit more at Barth's critique of the understanding of revelation and the theological method of what he refers to variously as liberalism, Cartesianism, neo-Protestantism, modernism, or anthropological theology. All of these terms refer to the modern theological tradition in which man is the "centre and measure and goal of all things."[6] At every point in this theology, man and the human situation is the starting point of theological thought in the attempt to understand God and revelation. Barth locates the influential origin of this theological method in medieval mysticism and the humanism of the Renaissance.[7] It receives classical expression in Descartes (1596–1650), who based the certainty of the existence of God on man's certainty of his own existence. It is also evident in the rationalism of Protestant orthodoxy. It comes to full flower in Protestantism following the Enlightenment, in the anthropological and humanistic theology of the nineteenth century. It reaches its zenith in Schleiermacher and his followers, and its denouement in Feuerbach, Harnack, and Troeltsch.[8]

We have noted that Barth's opposition to this modern Protestant tradition is evident in its essentials long before he began to write the *Church Dogmatics*. A statement from Barth's lecture on the "Humanity of God" delivered in 1956 provides the rationale for his dissatisfaction with this prevalent tradition.

Evangelical theology almost all along the line, certainly in all
its representative forms and tendencies, had become *religion-
istic, anthropocentric,* and in this sense *humanistic.* What I
mean to say is that an external and internal disposition and
emotion of man, namely his piety—which might well be Christian piety—had become its object of study and its theme.
Around this it revolved and seemed compelled to revolve
without release. . . . What did it know and say of the *deity* of
God? For this theology, to think about God meant to think in
a scarcely veiled fashion about man, more exactly about the
religious, the Christian religious man. To speak about God
meant to speak in an exalted tone but once again and more
than ever about this man—his revelations and wonders, his
faith and works. There is no question about it: here man was
made great at the cost of God—the divine God who is someone other than man, who sovereignly confronts him, who im-
movably and unchangeably stands over against him as the
Lord, Creator, and Redeemer.[9]

The traditional Roman Catholic interpretation of revelation, and the theological method connected with it, is the
second false position Barth opposes. Given Barth's earlier
opposition to Protestant liberalism and his understanding of
revelation, his attack upon Roman Catholicism at this point
was predictable. According to Roman Catholic dogma, the
teaching office of the Church is given the authority by Christ
to unfold the truths of revelation deposited in the Bible and
in the oral apostolic tradition. The chief error here lies not
only in the manner in which the Church possesses God's revelation, but also in the sovereign control she exercises over it.
Revelation is often conceived as a static deposit of truth
which requires only the infallible interpretation by the Church
in order to be regarded as a definitive truth or dogma. In
adopting this position, Rome fails to recognize that the
church's being is Jesus Christ, a "divine-human Person," and
is, therefore, "the action of God on man, an action in distinction from which human appropriation, as actually attested in
the very 'dogmas' believed in by the Church, may be termed
worthy, respectable, but by no means 'infallible,' and so not

withdrawn from further interrogation as to 'whether that is the relation.' "[10]

Barth regards both of these traditions as variants of what we have called anthropocentric theology. Their relationship should not be surprising, since Barth contends that the anthropological or humanistic perspective of neo-Protestantism has its roots in medieval Catholicism and not in the Reformers. Moreover, we shall see that the presuppositions used to support the development of a natural theology in Catholicism and neo-Protestantism are identical. In common with all other anthropological theologies, both attempt to establish a pathway to a knowledge of God which by-passes God's self-revelation in Jesus Christ. Barth's stand is unequivocal: "It is from the direction of Jesus Christ as the essence of the Church that we may expect free personal decision as to what ought to be the proper content of Christian language, and so also as to what should be the way to knowledge of it, to knowledge of dogma."[11] Both Roman Catholicism and Protestant liberalism in their understanding of revelation and theological methods fail to deal seriously enough with the fact that Jesus Christ as the center of God's revelation and so of the theological circle must be the referent to which every theological statement is related in some way. Barth's christocentric theology represents the attempt to fulfill this basic requirement of a Christian theology.

THE DOCTRINE OF THE WORD OF GOD: THE NORM OF CHRISTIAN THEOLOGY

Barth develops the massive prolegomena to his *Church Dogmatics* in terms of an exposition of "The Doctrine of the Word of God."[12] This is the larger framework within which— following Barth's order—we will consider the "Revelation of God" in terms of (1) "The Triune God," (2) "The Incarnation of the Word," and (3) "The Outpouring of the Holy Spirit." What Barth says in these areas constitutes the major portion of the two volumes of his prolegomena (C.D. I/1,

I/2). What he develops here is not just introductory to the positive content of Christian theology; rather, everything developed in the *Church Dogmatics* largely stands or falls on the basis of the fundamental positions which Barth develops in the above areas.

Although Barth's references to the Word of God are innumerable, he does not supply us with any one simple definition thereof. His reticence at this point is understandable, if we remember that the Word of God is synonymous with God's self-revelation. But the biblical God who reveals himself is never an object, thing, or *datum* under human control. God is like the bird in flight who cannot be captured even by the brush of the greatest artist. Thus every definition of the Word of God must acknowledge at the outset that God and his Word can be known by man only as God in his grace reveals himself.

The following recent statement concerning the Word of God typifies Barth's position:

> The Word of God is the Word that God *spoke, speaks,* and *will speak* in the midst of all men. Regardless of whether it is heard or not, it is, in itself, directed to all men. It is the Word of God's *work* upon men, for men, and with men. His work is not mute; rather, it speaks with a loud voice. Since only God can do what he does, only he can say in his work what he says. And since his work is not divided but *single* (for all the manifold forms which it assumes along the way from its origin to its goal), his Word is also (for all its exciting richness) simple and single. . . . God works, and since he works, he also speaks. His Word goes forth. . . . We are speaking of the God of the Gospel, his work and action, and of the Gospel in which his work and action are at the same time his speech. This is his Word, the Logos, in which the theological *logia,* logic, and language have their creative basis and life.[13]

In light of this statement, we are in a better position to appreciate Barth's exposition of the Word of God in terms of its threefold form in the opening pages of the *Church Dog-*

matics. He speaks of the Word of God which is preached, of the written Word of God in Holy Scripture, and finally, of the revealed Word of God which, in its fullest form, is Jesus Christ. Although Barth often speaks of the preached, written, and revealed Word of God in that sequence, his meaning becomes more clear if we deal first with the revealed Word of God.

The Revealed Word of God, Jesus Christ

It is characteristic of Barth to concentrate upon the incarnate Word, Jesus Christ, when speaking of the primary form of revelation or of the Word of God. Following the lead of the New Testament (John 1:1, 14; Heb. 1:2; Rev. 19:13), he feels it legitimate to identify the revealed Word of God in its highest expression with Jesus Christ. Thus he can write:

> Revelation in fact does not differ from the Person of Jesus Christ, and again does not differ from the reconciliation that took place in Him. To say revelation is to say 'The Word became flesh.'[14]

We would misconstrue Barth's christocentric doctrine of the Word of God, however, were we to interpret him to mean that the only form of the Word of God is the incarnate Word. He is at pains to make this point in this recent statement:

> The whole Word of God in Christ is the word to which theology must listen and reply. It is God's Word spoken both in the relation of the history of Israel to the history of Jesus Christ and in the relation of the history of Jesus Christ to the history of Israel. . . .

> Theology would not respond to the whole Word of God if it wished only to hear and to speak of the Word become flesh. . . . As if the reconciliation of the world with God were made at the expense of, or in abstraction from, the promises given to Israel![15]

If we keep this comprehensive definition of the Word of God in mind, the way in which Barth locates the center of God's self-revelation in Jesus Christ can hardly be faulted. Although Barth also speaks of the written and preached Word of God, they are its secondary forms. Both Scripture and proclamation become the Word of God through God's gracious action and presence in his Spirit, but they are secondary forms because they are essentially pointers to the concrete acts of God in the covenant history culminating in Jesus Christ.

The Written Word of God, Holy Scripture

The second form of the Word of God is Holy Scripture. For Barth, the biblical writers of the Old and New Testaments occupy a place of special authority in the church because they are the primary witnesses to God's mighty acts of revelation. ". . . they are called directly by the Word to be its hearers, and they are appointed for its communication and verification to other men." [16] It is through the witness of the Bible that all subsequent generations learn of God's acts. The Bible itself is not the primary form of revelation but it contains the testimony of the primary witnesses to God's revelation. It "is the concrete medium by which the Church recalls God's revelation in the past, is called to expect revelation in the future, and is thereby challenged, empowered, and guided to proclaim." [17]

Thus Barth is always careful to distinguish God in his revelation from the testimony to that revelation which confronts us in the Scriptures. In spite of his concern to reaffirm the primary authority of the Scriptures for the church as did the Reformers in their day, like them he does not intend to encourage bibliolatry! The first article of the "Theological Declaration" set forth at the Synod of Barmen in 1934 by the Confessing Church of Germany represents Barth's consistent position in this regard: "Jesus Christ, as He is attested to us in Holy Scripture, is the one Word of God, whom we have to hear and whom we have to trust and obey in life and in death." [18]

In what way, then, is Barth able to speak of Holy Scripture as the Word of God? How does this human and fallible witness of the prophets and apostles become the Word of God? Again, Barth's answer is always consistent: "The Bible is God's Word so far as God lets it be His Word, so far as God speaks through it." [19] In a subsequent section dealing with the doctrine of Holy Scripture, Barth clarifies his meaning by saying: "Scripture is holy and the Word of God, because by the Holy Spirit it became and will become to the Church a witness to divine revelation." [20] Thus, when God, who in his Spirit inspired the biblical writers, makes himself present in their testimony through his Spirit once again, we can confess that the Bible is the Word of God. This means that to understand the Bible and its relationship to God's revelation we must recognize both its humanity and its divinity, even as we acknowledge both in Jesus Christ. Barth writes:

> If we want to think of the Bible as a real witness of divine revelation, then clearly we have to keep two things constantly before us and give them their due weight; the limitation and the positive element, its distinctiveness from revelation, in so far as it is only a human word about it, and its unity with it, in so far as revelation is the basis, object and content of this word. [21]

The foregoing statement indicates quite clearly why Barth posits such a close correlation between Holy Scripture as the written Word of God and the revelation of God to which it points. The fact that Barth sees the Holy Spirit active both in the inspiration of the biblical writers and in making their witness a living Word of God through the ages accounts for his positive appreciation of the doctrine of the authority of Holy Scripture developed by the Reformers and held subsequently by Protestant Orthodoxy. However, he is critical of the development of the post-Reformation doctrine of the infallibility of the Scriptures in Protestant Orthodoxy. In its attempt to secure the authority of Holy Scripture against all detractors, Orthodoxy moved in the direction of equating Scripture—without any qualification—with the Word of God. By presuming that the Scriptures must provide a "divine and infallible history," Orthodoxy transformed the Scriptures from a witness to revelation into a doctrinal sourcebook. In so doing, the rigid and rationalistic orthodox doctrine of inspiration denied, in effect, the lordship of God over the biblical witnesses.

The orthodox attempt to secure the authority of the Scriptures by a high view of inspiration failed because it misconstrued the nature of the Bible and did not account for its humanity and therewith its fallibility. As such, it marked a retrogression from the adequate doctrine of the inspiration and authority of Holy Scripture held by Luther and Calvin. "For them," Barth writes, "the literally inspired Bible was not at all a revealed book of oracles, but a witness to revelation, to be interpreted from the standpoint of and with a view to its theme, and in conformity with that theme." [22] Protestant Orthodoxy's view of inspiration, however, moved in the direction of venerating a "paper Pope." Barth concluded: It "asserted things which cannot be maintained in face of a serious reading and exposition of what the Bible itself says about itself, and in face of an honest appreciation of the facts of its origin and tradition." [23]

In spite of Barth's dissatisfaction with the form of the orthodox Protestant doctrine of inspiration, he remained sympathetic both with its intention to affirm the authority of the Scriptures and with certain aspects of its hermeneutic. Modern Protestantism following the Enlightenment completely lost sight of the centrality of Holy Scripture. This eclipse marked in Barth's view one of the most lamentable epochs in the history of theology and of Protestantism in particular. Writing in 1939, however, Barth could affirm that this flagrant undermining of a basic tenet of the Reformation appeared to be passing. He saw the demise of neo-Protestantism being effected, in part, because it "is no longer able to satisfy the essence and obligation of this Church and theology as seen from the standpoint of Scripture and the Reformation itself."[24]

The Preached Word of God

The proclaimed or preached Word of God is the third and final form of the Word of God we need to consider. Once again, Barth builds on the conception of preaching as a form of the Word of God dominant in the Reformers and especially in Luther. By looking at two programmatic statements concerning preaching developed in the prolegomena, Barth's position becomes evident:

> The language about God to be found in the Church is meant to be proclamation, so far as it is directed towards man in the form of preaching and sacrament, with the claim and in an atmosphere of expectation that in accordance with its commission it has to tell him the Word of God to be heard in faith.[25]

> The Word of God is God Himself in the proclamation of the Church of Jesus Christ. In so far as God gives the Church the commission to speak about Him, and the Church discharges this commission, it is God Himself who declares His revelation in His witnesses. The proclamation of the Church is pure doctrine when the human word spoken in it in confirmation of the biblical witness to revelation offers and creates obedience to the Word of God.[26]

There are several important elements which need to be noted in Barth's view of preaching. First, although there are many ways in which the church may speak about God, preaching and sacrament occupy a distinctive place because the church is commissioned by Jesus Christ to proclaim the revelation of God through these two means. Barth defines preaching as the attempt, essayed by one called thereto in the Church, to express in his own words in the form of an exposition of a portion of the biblical testimony to revelation, and to make comprehensible to men of his day, the promise of God's revelation, reconciliation and calling, as they are to be expected here and now.[27]

Second, preaching—if it is to be true preaching—must be subservient to the Word of God attested in Holy Scripture and to nothing else. From this perspective, Barth finds both the Roman Catholic and neo-Protestant views of preaching deficient. The former has customarily relegated preaching to a secondary role because of the primacy of the sacrament as the medium through which God's grace is dispensed to the faithful. Barth does not deny that God may be present in the sacraments of the church, but he opposes the traditional Roman view of the sacrament because "grace neither is and remains here the personal free Word of God."[28] On the other hand, Protestant liberalism moves in the direction of subjectivism by conceiving preaching to be the unfolding of the piety of the preacher. This equation of preaching with "self-exposition" means its dissolution. Here the preacher no longer needs to listen to Scripture's testimony to God's self-revelation; in the last analysis, therefore, liberalism has no conception of preaching becoming the Word of God through God's gracious presence.

In the third place, even as the Scriptures become the Word of God in the event of God's presence in them through his Spirit, so also the human words of the preacher become from time to time the living Word of God. The miracle of God's presence in the world is not to be located in the physical transformation of the bread and the wine into the body and blood of our Lord as taught in the Roman Church. Rather, according to God's good pleasure he sanctifies, as it were, the words of his servants so that while remaining human words, they at the same time become words "in which and through which God Himself speaks about Himself."[29]

It is important to conclude this section by emphasizing that Barth is affirming that the one Word of God meets us in these three forms: there are not three Words of God. Though Barth does say that revelation gives rise to the other two forms of the Word of God which attest it, we never know of the former apart from Scripture and proclamation. Barth can therefore summarize the relationships obtaining between the three forms of the one Word of God as follows:

> The *revealed* Word of God we know only from the Scripture adopted by Church proclamation, or from Church proclamation based on Scripture. The *written* Word of God we know only through the revelation which makes proclamation possible, or through the proclamation made possible by revelation. The *proclaimed* Word of God we know only by knowing the revelation attested through Scripture, or by knowing Scripture which attests revelation.[30]

In a later section we will deal with the manner in which man appropriates the Word of God in faith. Here it must suffice to say that we can have no knowledge of God's revelation other than that which is mediated through the creaturely and worldly forms of Scripture and proclamation. Our knowledge of revelation "is only indirect, arising out of Scripture or in proclamation."[31]

THE REVELATION OF GOD

The entire discussion in this chapter to this point is already an analysis of Barth's understanding of revelation. Our purpose in the concluding sections is to analyze the content and nature of revelation somewhat more fully.

We have seen that to understand Barth's conception of the Word of God is to understand what he means by revelation. Moreover, it was noted in the section on "The Revealed Word of God, Jesus Christ," that the incarnation is the primary form of the Word of God and therefore of revelation. Our

earlier discussion also should have made clear that when
Barth speaks of the Christian understanding of revelation in
terms of the Word of God and of Jesus Christ, the Word
made flesh, he intends to distinguish Christian revelation from
all other real or supposed revelations. Unlike many modern
theologians who attempt to subsume the biblical understanding of revelation and of God beneath some more comprehensive or general conception of revelation or of ultimate Being,
Barth consistently affirms the uniqueness of the biblical
understanding of revelation and of the God who reveals himself in his revelation. His predilection is to begin with the
actual and concrete self-manifestation of God. Therefore, he
rejects beginning with a conception of revelation determined
by philosophy, metaphysics, philosophy of religion, comparative religion, or by any other conceptual schematism devised
by man.

What one writer has called Barth's "pathos for reality" is
apparent in these words about revelation:

> Knowledge of revelation does not mean an abstract knowledge
> of a God confronting an abstract man. Rather, it is a concrete
> knowledge of *the* God who has sought man and meets him in
> his concrete situation and finds him there. Revelation is a
> concrete knowledge of God and man in the event brought
> about by the initiative of a sovereign God.[32]

All of the aforementioned conceptions of revelation are faulty
since they are attempts to determine who God is in his revelation without looking at the actual form which his self-revelation takes.

What we have said thus far concerning the nature of God's
revelation may be summarized in Barth's recurring phrase,
"Through God alone may God be known." Only God can
reveal himself. He alone determines when, where, and how
he will manifest himself; moreover, he determines the conditions under which he may be known by man. Thus, every true
apprehension of God acknowledges that God in himself is
ultimate reality.

Whenever God reveals himself, he remains the free Lord. This means that "the very definite order of being which Holy Scripture makes manifest, when in its witness to God's revelation it confronts and relates God and man, divine facts and human attitudes, enforces an order of knowing corresponding to it." [33] It also means that man cannot speak and think as though he stood at some point which enabled him to determine what revelation should be or must be in advance of being encountered by God in his revelation. Any such position, which allows man to adopt a point "midway between God and man," is based upon a "twofold illusion and assumption": first, "the claim to know what God can and must do, to know what is necessary and appropriate to us men so that revelation between Him and us can become an event..."; and secondly, the "claim to know our own needs and possibilities." [34] Yet precisely such an approach characterizes the anthropological theology which invaded Protestant theology beginning about 1700, becoming dominant in the nineteenth century. Barth's critique of this tradition—which also intended to speak about revelation—is sharp: "Where a man becomes so arbitrary, where he has assumed this role of judge, whatever his verdict may be, he has nothing to do with God or the God-created fact of revelation." [35] In opposition to this approach, Barth proposes the following: "Divine determination and revelation, and not man's approval, are the criterion of what is appropriate to God and salutary for us." [36]

The Triune God

Part I of Barth's doctrine of revelation is entitled "The Triune God" [37] (C.D. I/1, §8-12). In developing the doctrine of revelation in terms of the doctrine of the Trinity, Barth departed radically from the customary procedure in modern theology in at least three points. First, he made the doctrine of the Trinity the key to understanding the Christian conception of revelation and of God. Second, Barth treats this doctrine in the prolegomena and prior to the subsequent development of the doctrine of God. Third, he resuscitated a doctrine which had received only cursory attention in Protestant liberalism since Schleiermacher, and developed a doctrine of the Trinity which is indubitably the "greatest treatise on the Trinity since the Reformation."[38]

Barth's attempt to interpret the revelation of God in terms of the doctrine of the Trinity is set forth in the following thesis:

> God's Word is God Himself in His revelation. For God reveals Himself as the Lord and that according to Scripture signifies for the concept of revelation that God Himself in unimpaired unity yet also in unimpaired difference is Revealer, Revelation, and Revealedness.[39]

The basic reason why Barth expounds the doctrine of revelation in terms of the doctrine of the Trinity is that the answer to the question, "Who is the God who reveals himself?" points in this direction. He writes: "We have to do with the concept of the revelation of the God who, according to Scripture and proclamation, is the Father of Jesus Christ, is Jesus Christ Himself, is the Spirit of this Father and of this Son."[40] We are forbidden, therefore, if we wish to speak about the triune God of the Bible, to begin with some general doctrine of God or of ultimate Being abstracted from God the Father who makes himself known in his Son and through his Spirit. Nor is it possible to arrive at an understanding of God as triune by reasoning from analogies of the Trinity which may be found in nature, culture, history, or human existence (*vestigia trinitatis*). This is another form of natural theology, representing man's projections. Barth does not contend that the doctrine of the Trinity is to be found in the Bible; he maintains, however, that an investigation of the unity and diversity between the ways in which God reveals himself brings us "up against the problem of the doctrine of the Trinity."[41] Or he can say that the biblical witness to revelation is the "root" or "ground" of the doctrine of the Trinity.[42]

In contradistinction to Schleiermacher, who relegated the

doctrine of the Trinity to the end of his Dogmatics because it was speculative and did not represent an immediate implication of the Christian's self-consciousness, and in opposition to most of his followers who regarded it as a speculative doctrine somewhat peripheral in Christian theology, Barth's stand is unequivocal:

> It is the doctrine of the Trinity which fundamentally distinguishes the Christian doctrine of God as Christian—it is it, therefore, also, which marks off the Christian concept of revelation as Christian, in face of all other possible doctrines of God and concepts of revelation.[43]

This survey of Barth's doctrine of revelation necessitates the briefest résumé of some of the features of his doctrine of the Trinity. The wealth of exegetical and historical material which undergirds his conclusions must be left to the reader's careful scrutiny. We must restrict ourselves to singling out a few significant positions established in the gradual development of the doctrine of the Trinity which are crucial for Barth's view as well. In the first place, it is important to note that the doctrine of the Trinity was precipitated by the confession of Jesus Christ as Lord in the New Testament. Thus the church acknowledged God to be present in Jesus; in the Son, God determined to be present in yet another form. The early church was right in distinguishing the Son from the Father while at the same time recognizing that he was one with the Father in terms of his essential nature or essence. Subsequently, the church affirmed that God was present in yet another form in the Holy Spirit. Here, too, the one God was present yet again.

In agreement with the early church, Barth affirms the necessity of maintaining—in light of the scriptural evidence—at least two important truths concerning the nature of God's self-revelation in the Son and in the Spirit. First, all subordinationism is ruled out. Neither the Son nor the Spirit are subordinate in rank to the Father. We are not confronted

with some semidivine beings in the Son and the Spirit. Rather,
the one God confronts us in these different modes of his being.
It is absolutely essential for interpreting Barth to emphasize
his insistence that in the various modes of God's being in his
revelation in history we are met with none other than *God
himself!* Otherwise we would be forced to admit that in the
Son and the Spirit we encounter someone less than God.
Were this the case, we could not speak of any real revelation
or unveiling of God. Second, Barth rejects the kind of modal-
ism evident in the early church which held that God's self-
manifestation in the Son and the Spirit represent only temporary roles which God assumes. The true God—they held—
is hidden from us and exists beyond these temporary roles
which he assumes in accommodating himself to us. To accede
to this view once again calls revelation into question; it denies
that we are really met by God in his revelation.

It remains for us to look at some of the elements which
must be included in the doctrine of the Trinity. The following
summary statement provides an outline for our discussion:

> We mean by the doctrine of the Trinity, in a general and pre-
> liminary way, the proposition that He whom the Christian
> Church calls God and proclaims as God, therefore the God
> who has revealed Himself according to the witness of Scrip-
> ture, is the same in unimpaired unity, yet also the same in
> unimpaired variety thrice in a different way. Or, in the
> phraseology of the dogma of the Trinity in the Church, the
> Father, the Son and the Holy Spirit in the Bible's witness to
> revelation are the one God in the unity of their essence, and
> the one God in the Bible's witness to revelation is in the va-
> riety of His Persons the Father, the Son, and the Holy Spirit.[44]

Barth's discussion of the Trinity underlines the following
propositions:

(1) God is one in his essential being or substance (essence)
or nature. In no way will Barth admit the charge that the
doctrine of the Trinity moves in the direction of tritheism.
Above all, it underlines the oneness and unity of God. There

is one divine essence, not three. To be sure, the church doctrine of the Trinity maintains that this is a unique oneness; it is a "oneness in threeness" as Barth puts it. Or we can say, it affirms a triunity in the Godhead.

(2) In agreement with the traditional doctrine of the Trinity, Barth asserts that there are three persons, subsistencies, or modes in the one being of God. Barth writes: "God ... is One in three of His modes of existence, which consist in their mutual relationships, Father, Son and Holy Spirit." [45] There is a "threeness" in the oneness of God. God, therefore, has a rich, inner life in terms of the interrelationships of the three modes of his one being. He is tripersonal or "tri-une." The basis for maintaining that there are distinctions in the Godhead—i.e., modes of God's being—is based on the fact that the one God reveals himself thrice as Father, Son, and Holy Spirit. Barth can refer to this as God's "threefold repetition" of himself.[46] These distinctions which mark God's revelation and repetition of himself (economic trinity) point to distinctions within the Godhead (immanent or ontological Trinity). Thus the threeness which is visible in God's revelation is a reflection of the triunity or the threeness which is integral to his nature as God. Were this not so we would be forced once more to say that God is different from that which he reveals himself to be.

Since the traditional term "person" describing the different ways God has revealed himself is often misconstrued in a tritheistic sense—contrary to its original meaning—Barth prefers to speak of the three "modes" of God's one being in order to say the same thing more clearly. He writes:

> The statement "God is one in three modes of being, Father, Son, and Holy Spirit" thus means that the one God, i.e., the one Lord, the One personal God is what He is not in one mode only, but—we appeal in support simply to the results of our analysis of the Biblical content of revelation—in the mode of the Father, in the mode of the Son, in the mode of the Holy Spirit.[47]

We may summarize these two essential theses in the doctrine of the Trinity by saying that we must affirm the "oneness in threeness" in God's revelation of himself. We must also stress the "threeness in oneness" in order to point to the distinctions in the Godhead and in revelation. Finally, Barth conflates these two theses and speaks of a "three-in-oneness" in God.[48]

(3) The whole undivided essence of God belongs equally to each of the three modes of God's being. It is therefore illegitimate to regard the essence of God as divided among the modes of his being or to see a diminution of the essence of God the Father in the Son and the Spirit. The only subordination of which Barth speaks relates to the order of relationships within the Godhead and therewith in the modes of God's being. This means that there is a "mutual interpenetration" or a mutual indwelling of the three modes of God's being. This is another way of affirming with the ancient church that God is fully present in each of the modes of his being. Thus, for example, even when we attribute creation to the Father, reconciliation to the Son, and sanctification to the Spirit, this in no way means that only a part of God is present in each of these modes. We make these distinctions in order to describe God's revelation while remembering that the one God is fully present in each of the modes of his being, even as they coexist and interpenetrate each other in the Godhead.

(4) Barth is quite conscious that all theological formulations are inadequate to plumb, for example, the nature of the three-in-oneness of the divine Godhead. However, the doctrine of the Trinity is the church's attempt to understand, in so far as possible, the nature of God. Ultimately, we cannot know God as he knows himself. Yet Barth maintains that the language of the doctrine of the Trinity may be analogous to its object, God, and therefore "not without truth."[49]

Barth's concluding words on the "Meaning of the Doctrine of the Trinity" provide a suitable conclusion to our discussion:

> The doctrine of the Trinity declares—and that is the positive point it stands up for on its fighting front—that and how far

He who reveals Himself to man according to the witness of Scripture can be our *God,* that and how far He can be *our* God. He can be our *God,* because He is equal to Himself in all His modes of existence, is one and the same Lord. Knowledge of revelation, as it may arise on the witness of Scripture, means, in terms of the doctrine of the Trinity, in all elements of the event to which this witness points us, knowledge of the Lord as Him who meets us and unites us to Himself. And this Lord can be *our* God, He can meet us and unite us to Himself, because He is God in these three modes of existence as Father, Son, and Spirit, because creation, reconciliation, redemption, the entire being, language, and action in which He wills to be our God, is grounded and typified in His own essence, in His Godness itself.[50]

The Incarnation of the Word: The Objective Revelation of God

The first part of Barth's doctrine of revelation is his massive exposition of the doctrine of the Trinity. We have followed that order because the answer to the question concerning the nature of the God who reveals himself is essential to everything which is said about him. Now we must turn to the further exposition of Barth's doctrine of revelation (C.D. I/2) developed under the headings "The Incarnation of the Word" (Part II) and "The Outpouring of the Holy Spirit" (Part III). In doing so, we are not turning to some other revelation than that spoken of up to this point. Rather, our attention is directed more precisely to the manner in which Jesus Christ is the "objective reality and possibility" of revelation; that is, how Jesus Christ is *God's* revelation for us. The work of God as Holy Spirit is the subject of the next section. There our concern will be to analyze how Barth conceives of man's subjective reception of God's revelation or of "God's revelation in us."

By now it should be apparent why Barth begins by discussing the "reality" of God's revelation in Jesus Christ before turning to its "possibility." That is to say, we must begin with the concrete revelation of God in Jesus Christ as the manner in which *God* is free for man. We are forbidden to begin with

the questions "Is there a God?" "Is revelation possible?" or
"What are the human conditions which need to be fulfilled if
God is to reveal himself?" This is to begin anthropologically
rather than christologically; it allows man to determine the
conditions under which God will reveal himself. Barth re-
verses the customary procedure of much recent Protestant
theology by beginning with the actuality and reality of the
revelation of God in Jesus Christ. Subsequently, he turns to
the question concerning Jesus Christ as the objective "possibility" of revelation. Here we have moved from the question
of fact to that of interpretation. It is not a matter of asking
whether revelation has taken place in Jesus Christ; it is rather
the attempt to understand the extent to which the revelation
of God in Jesus Christ is God's revelation *to man*. To ask
about the possibility of revelation subsequent to asking about
its reality means that we are to read off its possibility from
its actuality. Here, as in all theology, it is a matter of faith
seeking further understanding and illumination concerning
the event of revelation.[51]

In turning to Barth's interpretation of revelation in terms
of the doctrine of the incarnation, we are not to expect the
full development of his christology. Here Barth concentrates
on the manner in which God is present and free for man in
Jesus Christ. We do well to cite his thematic statement in full:

> According to Holy Scripture God's revelation takes place in
> the fact that God's Word became a man and that this man has
> become God's Word. The incarnation of the eternal Word,
> Jesus Christ, is God's revelation. In the reality of this event
> God proves that he is free to be our God.[52]

The primary point of this entire section is that the "objective reality" of God's revelation to us and for us is identical
with the historical person, Jesus Christ, including his incarnation, life, death, and resurrection. Barth summarizes the witness
of the New Testament to the reality of God's revelation in
Jesus Christ in this twofold statement: "The Word or Son of
God became a Man and was called Jesus of Nazareth; there-

fore this Man Jesus of Nazareth was God's Word or God's Son."[53] This summary statement is the basis for the affirmation of the God-manhood of Jesus Christ and as such is another way of affirming with the early church that Jesus Christ was "truly God" and "truly man." The first of the christologies represented, i.e., that which speaks of the Word of God becoming the man Jesus, is the Johannine. Here the movement in speaking about revelation is from above to below; that is, the eternal Word became a man, Jesus. The Synoptics move from below to above: the man Jesus of Nazareth is God's Son.

Barth reiterates that there is no possibility of acknowledging the deity of Jesus Christ if—in the tradition of much modern Protestant theology—one begins with a preconceived notion of God, of the nature of incarnation, of divinity, or of the Son or Word of God, and then proceeds to find this conception filled in Jesus. To fall prey to this approach means to succumb to docetism; here one does not take the reality of Jesus' humanity with utmost seriousness. One can know that God was present in Jesus Christ only by looking at the person of Jesus; he alone determines what incarnation means. Only by looking at Jesus Christ do we confess with the New Testament that "the Word became flesh" (John 1:14, RSV). Barth regards this Johannine confession as the guide for understanding that Jesus Christ is both and at the same time "very God and very man."[54]

With respect to the Synoptic confession that this man Jesus of Nazareth is the Son of God, Barth warns against the Ebionite misinterpretation of Jesus. This early christological heresy is repeated in some liberal Protestants who equate Jesus' divinity with the highest expression or development of human nature. The result is a deification of man, and we cannot speak of the real occurrence of revelation. The New Testament, on the contrary, even in the Synoptic christology, affirms that in this man, Jesus of Nazareth, men were encountered by the Son of God.

This twofold confession of Jesus Christ as the reality of

God's revelation of himself provides the basis for all dogmatic reflection about him. Barth summarizes: "God's freedom for us men is a fact in Jesus Christ, according to the
witness of Holy Scripture. The first and the last thing to
be said about the bearer of this name is that He is very God
and very Man. In this unity He is the objective reality of
divine revelation." [55]

On the basis of the reality of the revelation in Jesus Christ,
we are prepared with Barth to seek to discover how this reality
can be "God's revelation to man." [56] This is the question of
"Jesus Christ" as the "Objective Possibility of Revelation."
With this language Barth wishes to underline that apart from
Jesus Christ there is no possibility of true knowledge of God,
of man, or of their relationship to one another. He writes:

> Revelation itself is needed for knowing that God is hidden
> and man blind. Revelation and it alone really and finally sep-
> arates God and man by bringing them together. For by bring-
> ing them together it informs man about God and about him-
> self, it reveals God as the Lord of eternity, as the Creator,
> Reconciler and Redeemer, and characterizes man as a crea-
> ture, as a sinner, as one devoted to death. It does that by tell-
> ing him that God is free for us, that God has created and
> sustains him, that He forgives his sin, that He saves him from
> death. But it tells him that this God (no other) is free for this
> man (no other). [57]

The possibility of revelation is grounded in the freedom of
God manifest in Jesus Christ. We can point to five things this
means for Barth. First, the reality of Jesus Christ means that
God is God "not only in Himself but also in and among us";
i.e., "that God can cross the boundary between Him and
us." [58] Here we are dealing with the mystery of the divine
condescension in the incarnation.

Second, the reality of Jesus Christ means that "God is free
for us, in the sense that He reveals Himself to us in such a
way that His Word or His Son becomes a man—not God the
Father, and not God the Holy Spirit." [59] Here Barth wants to

stress again that "God in His entire divinity became man." [60]

Third, the fact that God revealed himself in human flesh within human history means that "He can become cognizable by us by analogy with other forms known to us." [61] Elsewhere Barth can say that the fact that the Word became flesh is the "first, original, and dominating sign of all signs." [62] Beginning with the humanity of Jesus Christ, God has ordained that certain objects of the created world should become the means of effecting a relationship with himself. Here we recall what Barth said about the written and the preached Word of God which point us to the primary sign, Jesus Christ. However, the fact that God in love makes himself knowable in the humanity of Jesus Christ is pure grace; because of man's sin, we cannot reason from the creature and the creaturely to the Creator.

Fourth, even though the Word becomes man in Jesus Christ, this is not to be interpreted as a condescension (*kenosis*) in which God ceases to be God. "By becoming flesh the Word is no less true and entire God than He was previously in eternity in Himself." [63]

Finally, the reality of God's revelation in Jesus Christ "becomes possible in such a way that God's Son or Word becomes Man. He does not become any kind of natural being. He becomes what we ourselves are." [64] That God becomes man is his free choice. We could not argue for the necessity of incarnation because humanity has a latent capacity to reveal God. We know what it means to be man by looking at the humanity of Jesus Christ; we see that we are beings who are created and sustained by him. Even more, in taking our sinful humanity upon himself, the Son has taken the "entire curse of sin" upon himself.

THE TIME OF REVELATION

A brief word must suffice concerning Barth's exposition of "The Time of Revelation." The lead statement is as follows:

> God's revelation in the event of the presence of Jesus Christ is God's time for us. It is fulfilled time in this event itself.

But as the Old Testament time of expectation and as the New
Testament time of recollection it is also the time of witness to
this event.[65]

Certain features stand out in Barth's exposition to which
we can only direct attention. Another way to express the
meaning of God's revelation in Jesus Christ is to say that
God has time for man. Moreover, time and history must be
interpreted in the light of revelation and not vice versa. This
leads Barth to say that our finite and fallen time must now be
viewed in terms of the event of Jesus Christ who is the manifestation of the time of revelation, and therefore of real or
fulfilled time. However, as we noted earlier, Jesus Christ
cannot be understood apart from the covenant which preceded him. Or better: the Old Testament "time of expectation"—the "pre-time to revelation"—cannot be understood
apart from its fulfillment in Jesus Christ. Thus the Old Testament witnesses to the expected and coming revelation. On
the other hand, the time of the New Testament witness is also
intimately related to the fulfilled time of Jesus Christ. "This
subsequent time is the time of the New Testament, or the
time of the witness to recollection of revelation."[66] By arguing
in this manner, Barth makes the revelation of God in Jesus
Christ constitutive for interpreting the two covenants, in terms
both of their differences and of their underlying unity. The
fact that the Son was God's revelation in time is hidden in
the event of the cross, but manifest in his resurrection from
the dead. That crucial event is the basis for the Christian hope
and the eschatological perspective of the New Testament which
looks toward his coming again.[67] In his anthropology, Barth
draws out further some of the implications of this christocentric perspective on time. We can cite only the introductory
thesis:

Man lives in the allotted span of his present, past and future
life. He who was before him and will be after him, and who

therefore fixes the boundaries of his being, is the eternal God, his Creator, and Covenant-partner. He is the hope in which man may live in his time.[68]

THE MYSTERY OF REVELATION

The lines of Barth's christology are amplified in his treatment of the incarnation as that which points to the mystery of revelation. As we have seen, Barth begins and ends all of his discussions about revelation and christology by affirming with the early church and the Council of Chalcedon (A.D. 451) that the *content* of the incarnation must be understood in terms of the divine and human natures which were united in the one person, Jesus Christ. He puts it this way:

> The mystery of the revelation of God in Jesus Christ consists in the fact that the eternal Word of God chose, sanctified and assumed human nature and existence into oneness with Himself, in order thus, as very God and very man, to become the Word of reconciliation spoken by God to man.[69]

THE MIRACLE OF CHRISTMAS

Barth concludes his treatment of Jesus Christ as the incarnation of the Word of God and therewith God's objective revelation to man with a strong defense of the doctrine of the Virgin Birth. This dogma of the early church points to the "miracle of Christmas." Its concern is with the form in which God's revelation comes to us. The doctrine of the Virgin Birth is the sign which points to the mystery of the revelation of God in Jesus Christ, the Word of God become flesh. This doctrine emphasizes that the God-manhood of Jesus Christ is a mystery which can only be confessed. It cannot be comprehended intellectually. Further, it accentuates the fact that God alone is the active author who effects the incarnation. This excludes the kind of synergism which regards man as God's coworker in the incarnation. Yet the fact that Jesus is born of the Virgin Mary is at the same time the sign that God

"justifies and sanctifies human nature in spite of its unright-
eousness and unholiness to be a temple for His Word." [70] We
can summarize Barth's position with his words:

> The sign of this mystery [i.e., of the incarnation] revealed
> in the resurrection of Jesus Christ is the miracle of His birth,
> that He was conceived by the Holy Ghost, born of the Virgin
> Mary. [71]

The Outpouring of the Holy Spirit: The Subjective Revelation of God

We have traversed a long road to this point in our chapter.
Major attention in developing Barth's understanding of revelation has been given to (1) his doctrine of the Word of God.
Then we considered the nature of the God who reveals himself
in terms of (2) the doctrine of the Trinity. In the preceding
section, we gave more specific attention to (3) the objective
event in which God is free for us, namely, the incarnation of
the Word of God. This provided an insight into the main lines
of Barth's christology. Now (4) we must look at the way in
which God's revelation in Jesus Christ is appropriated by
man. This leads us to the subjective pole of Barth's doctrine
of revelation and therewith to his pneumatology.

SOME FALSE APPROACHES

The reader of the early Barth may have anticipated his
treatment of the work of the Holy Spirit in the *Church Dogmatics* with some scepticism. He may recall Barth's trenchant
critique of the prevailing piety of neo-Protestantism with its
concentration upon Christian experience to the neglect of the
objective activity of God in revelation. This accounts for the
wholesale repudiation of mysticism in all its forms by the
dialectical theologians in the twenties. In 1924 Emil Brunner
wrote a book denouncing Schleiermacher and his followers
for transforming the Christian faith into an illicit mysticism.
In adopting this stance, the dialectical theologians were following in the train of Albrecht Ritschl (1822–1889) who in

his own way emphasized the revelation in Jesus Christ and the kingdom of God in opposition to Protestant pietism which focused attention on the individual's subjective religious experience.[72]

Barth's approach to man's appropriation of revelation is evident in the first half-volume of the *Church Dogmatics* published in 1932. In speaking of the "Word of God and Experience" he observed that the emphasis of the nineteenth century on "man's religious consciousness" need not be repudiated if properly understood. For Barth this meant—and herein he never changed his position—the following: "By experience of the Word of God . . . we understand the determination of their existence as men by the Word of God."[73] Thus as long as we understand that man's faith and therewith his experience always must be viewed in terms of God's activity in his life enabling him to believe, we will be on the right track.[74]

On the basis of Barth's doctrine of revelation, his subsequent attack upon the "self-centered I-piety" characteristic of the hymnody of neo-Protestantism and pietism is quite consistent. In contrast to Reformation hymnody which praised God for his saving acts, modern Protestantism is obsessed with the "gurgling gullet of modern religious self-confession."[75] In a later reference to this critique, Barth maintains that it was necessary as a "counterblast to the general subjectivist trend of modern Protestantism." However, he continues: "But as is obvious from the presence of the I-Psalms in the Bible, it can only be a relative and not an absolute criticism."[76] Statements from the later volumes of the *Church Dogmatics* appear to substantiate Barth's intention from the outset to accord the subjective apprehension of revelation its rightful place in his dogmatics; nevertheless, he admits to a deeper understanding of the experiential dimension of faith in these later volumes than he had in his earlier writings.[77]

In addition to the aforementioned deficiencies which Barth notes in the subjectivism of much modern Protestantism, we must mention yet another. He dissociates himself from the

manner in which Protestant pietists described the exact way
in which man apprehends God's revelation, and the subjective
states and moods connected therewith. Here again Barth hesi-
tates to say anything specific concerning the way in which
man "experiences" the Holy Spirit, because Holy Scripture
gives no help at this juncture. He is satisfied to say that both
the objective revelation of God in Jesus Christ and the subjective appropriation thereof through the work of the Holy
Spirit are manifestations of God's grace. "What lies between
them we can never express or state, because it is not revealed
to us. And it is not revealed to us because it is revelation
itself." [78]

A final opponent which is always in the background in
Barth's discussion of the appropriation of revelation is sectarianism. This tradition ordinarily understands the testimony of the Holy Spirit in terms of some "immediate spir-
itual inspiration" which "by-passes the Word and its testi-
monies." [79] To the extent that sectarianism is guilty of this
procedure, it must be opposed, since man's knowledge of
God is inviolable only as long as it is bound to the Word of
God and made known through the Holy Spirit.

It is important to keep these opponents in view, both for
understanding the position Barth is to develop and for seeing
him in the context of modern theology. The perennial danger
in theology according to Barth—and one which was not
avoided in modern Protestantism—is that man's reception of
revelation, and therewith his faith and piety, will be made
into an independent, or even central, theme in theology.
Though we have not done so, it would be quite accurate to
account for Barth's opposition to the theology of Rudolf
Bultmann on the grounds that it represents a contemporary
example of anthropological theology. [80]

In order to avoid this error, Barth urges that man's experience of faith be understood in the light of Jesus Christ, that
is, "in and by its source, in and by Jesus Christ as its basis,
upon which it is dependent but which is not dependent upon
it." [81] This means that man cannot become a believer apart

from the prior and continuing grace of God. Precisely at this point, Barth finds neo-Protestantism most vulnerable. It did not have a strong doctrine of man as sinner who through grace alone is made a participant in the act of revelation. As a consequence, it did not require a strong doctrine of the work of the Holy Spirit. Though it spoke of the work of the Spirit, Barth concludes that the Holy Spirit was not its real concern but rather "the spirit of human inwardness and seriousness, the spirit of mysticism and morals." [82] Here the human spirit, the spirit of man and humanity, is all that is required to speak of the knowledge of God. [83]

FAITH AND THE KNOWLEDGE OF GOD

We are now ready to see how man is made free for God in the thought of Barth. The major thesis which he develops in this section is the following:

> According to Holy Scripture God's revelation occurs in our enlightenment by the Holy Spirit of God to a knowledge of His Word. The outpouring of the Holy Spirit is God's revelation. In the reality of this event consists our freedom to be the children of God and to know and love and praise Him in His revelation. [84]

Barth's consideration of the subjective reception of God's revelation by man presupposes that Holy Scripture instructs us at this point. Therefore, any theology which talked about God's activity in Jesus Christ without dealing with man's appropriation of this revelation would be incomplete. Furthermore, men apprehend God's revelation not as isolated individuals but within the church, the Body of Christ, of which Christ is the head. The fact that such a community exists in the world is due to the outpouring of the Holy Spirit at Pentecost. Its continuation through the ages derives from God's continuing gracious manifestation of himself through various signs in the church—such as Scripture, preaching, and sacrament—which testify of Christ, the objective reality of revelation. Thus, Barth begins with the Holy Spirit, the subjective *reality* of revelation, who makes it possible for God to be known by his children in a particular community, namely, his church.[85] In talking about the reception of revelation, Barth once more begins by talking about what *God* does to mediate his presence to man through his Spirit. Barth summarizes his view concerning the work of the Holy Spirit as the "subjective reality" of revelation thus:

> The subjective reality of revelation consists in the fact that we have our being through Christ and in the Church, that we are the recipients of the divine testimonies, and, as the real recipients of them, the children of God. But the fact that we have this being is the work of the Holy Spirit. Therefore the Holy Spirit is the subjective reality of revelation.[86]

This leads us to the second question: how does the revelation of God "come into man?"[87] We noted earlier Barth's hesitancy concerning any description of "how" God works through his Spirit so that certain men believe in him. Even as we were unable to plumb the mystery of the God-manhood of Jesus Christ, so Holy Scripture does not enable us to unravel the mystery of God's presence with us and in us through his Spirit. Hence with respect to "the outpouring of the Holy Spirit by which the objective reality of revelation becomes a subjective reality," Barth suggests: "We have to respect the mystery of the given-ness of this fact as such, i.e., as the inconceivable and therefore the unspeakable mystery of the person and work of God."[88]

The only possible approach to the question concerning how the objective revelation of God in Jesus Christ becomes real for us, Barth states as follows:

> Subjective revelation can consist only in the fact that objective revelation, the one truth which cannot be added to or bypassed, comes to man and is recognised and acknowledged by man. And that is the work of the Holy Spirit. About that work there is nothing specific that we can say. We can speak

about it only by sheer repetition, that is, by repeating what is told us objectively, that "God was in Christ reconciling the world unto himself." The work of the Holy Spirit is that our blind eyes are opened and that thankfully and in thankful self-surrender we recognise and acknowledge that it is so: Amen. . . . Subjective revelation can be only the repetition, the impress, the sealing of objective revelation upon us; or, from our point of view, our own discovery, acknowledgment and affirmation of it. . . . when the Holy Spirit draws and takes us right into the reality of revelation by doing what we cannot do, by opening our eyes and ears and hearts, He does not tell us anything except that we are in Christ by Christ. Therefore we have to say, and in principle it is all that we can say, that we are brethren of the Son of God, hearers and doers of the Word of God.[89]

Barth stands squarely in the tradition of the Reformers in depicting man's freedom for God in terms of the work of the Holy Spirit. Hence, the "subjective possibility" of revelation is grounded in the work of the Holy Spirit. Once again, we move from the reality to the possibility; i.e., from what God does, to a consideration of what this means for our relationship to him. The possibility of man's freedom for God can be put thus:

It is real in the Holy Spirit that we are free for God. And this settles the fact that we are not free for God except in the Holy Spirit. The work of the Holy Spirit itself cuts away from us the thought of any other possibility of our freedom for God.[90]

Barth summarizes the positive meaning of man's freedom for God through the outpouring of the Holy Spirit in the following propositions: (1) "By the outpouring of the Holy Spirit it is possible for God's revelation to reach man in his freedom, because in it the Word of God is brought to his hearing." (2) Further, "by the outpouring of the Holy Spirit it is possible in the freedom of man for God's revelation to meet him, because in it he is explicitly told by God's Word that he possesses no possibility of his own for such a meeting." (3) "By the outpouring of the Holy Spirit it becomes possible for man in his freedom to be met by God's revelation, because in it the Word of God becomes unavoidably his master." [91]

The Reformers are also Barth's guides in his repeated emphasis upon the Holy Spirit as the "teacher of the Word" and therefore the source of all our knowledge of Jesus Christ and therewith of revelation. To speak about knowledge of Jesus Christ means for Barth to witness to the mystery and miracle of the gift and reception of the Holy Spirit.[92] We can speak of the Spirit of God as divine "in the fact that Jesus Christ is its power and light, its content, its origin and goal. It is the fulfillment of His self-witness." [93] This close correlation between the Spirit and the Son rules out confusing the Holy Spirit with some experience of the numinous, which, in fact, is more akin to the demonic than to the divine.[94]

It is only in and with the response of faith that it becomes possible to speak about man knowing God at all. Barth provides us with a further indication of his understanding of faith in these words: "The knowledge of God occurs in the fulfillment of the revelation of His Word by the Holy Spirit, and therefore in the reality and with the necessity of faith and its obedience." [95] Here and always when speaking about the relationship between God and man, the priority belongs to God. Accordingly, every discussion of faith which overlooks how God determines this relationship is speaking of something other than the biblical faith. Barth puts his point strongly in these words:

> Biblical faith excludes any faith of man in himself—that is, any desire for religious self-help, any religious self-satisfaction, any religious self-sufficiency. Biblical faith lives upon the objectivity of God. . . . God speaks; He claims; He promises; He acts; He is angry; He is gracious. Take away the objectivity of this *He*, and faith collapses, even as love, trust and obedience.[96]

Thus we need to keep in mind throughout our discussion of Barth's view of man's knowledge of God that man's faith is a sign of God's grace; it is not a human work or act which man can effect apart from God. When faith is present, a miracle has taken place.[97]

We probe more deeply in asking: what is the relationship between God and man, between the divine and human subjects, in the divine-human encounter? Barth is reticent to formulate a theory of knowledge which would in any way dictate how God must relate himself to man. However, he does utilize the subject/object schematism characteristic of philosophical discussion relating to man's knowledge of objects external to him. Readers of Barth acquainted with his untiring emphasis upon the fact that God is always the subject who acts may be unprepared for the way he stresses that God becomes an "object" in revelation. James Brown may be correct in characterizing Barth as the theologian for whom God is "indissolubly Subject," for whom, like Martin Buber, God never becomes merely an "it."[98] Yet Barth can describe the way in which God is known thus: "If God becomes the object of human knowledge in faith, that must mean that He becomes the object of human perception and comprehension."[99]

In addition, therefore, to being objective to himself (his primary "objectivity") in his triune being, there is the secondary objectivity of God—a "clothed objectivity"—which comes to us indirectly through the various creaturely media which God utilizes to make himself known.[100] In his primary objectivity, God always remains hidden from us. However, we have seen that God meets man as a "thou" in Jesus Christ, establishing by means of the humanity of Jesus Christ a reciprocal relationship between himself and man. Other creaturely media or signs such as preaching and sacraments become the channels by which he mediates himself indirectly. This is why the knowledge of faith is unique; it always stems from the divine election. It is dependent at every point upon the precedence of the divine grace. "Faith is simply following, following its object. Faith is going a way which is marked out and prepared."[101] This explains why man never gains control over God in his revelation, and ultimately this is why Barth designates the attitude of prayer as befitting one who truly desires to know God.[102]

The concept which Barth regards as most appropriate to express man's total participation in the experience of the Word of God is that of acknowledgment (*Anerkennung*). It is the most descriptive of what is involved in the divine-human encounter for several reasons. First, the word itself signifies a "rational event." Second, it suggests a relationship between persons. Third, it connotes the "acceptance" of what is acknowledged. Fourth, the concept of acknowledgment focuses attention on the fact that we are concerned with a real presence of God and not with the mere recollection of God in the past. Fifth, acknowledgment on man's part implies man's obedience to the Word of God. Sixth, the term accentuates that faith involves man's decision. Seventh, to speak of acknowledgment of God preserves the necessary respect for the mystery which always accompanies revelation. Finally, this word commends itself because it signifies a "movement" and never a static attitude of man.[103] Whenever Barth uses this concept, he intends to point to a unique kind of human knowledge: "It is recognition in the form of acknowledgment: recognition under the law of faith and obedience." [104]

The primarily noetic character of faith is visible in the three descriptive words which Barth chooses as the basis for his discussion of the "Act of Faith." He writes that Christian faith is "an acknowledgment (*Anerkennung*), a recognition (*Erkennen*), and a confession (*Bekennen*). As all these terms indicate, it is a knowledge." [105] Faith understood as acknowledgment is above all else a cognitive act in which man takes notice of the prior work and being of the living Christ. In the normal order of man's relationship with an object external to him, recognition precedes his acknowledgment. But in the faith moment the opposite is true: the act of acknowledgment is primary and the act of cognition flows from it as its necessary consequence. Concerning the priority of acknowledgment in the faith moment, Barth writes: "It [i.e., acknowledgment] is not preceded by any other kind of knowledge, either recognition or confession. The recognition and confession of faith are included in and follow from the fact that they are originally and properly an acknowledgment, the free act of obedience." [106]

The process of recognition is one in which faith becomes articulate or understood. This is the same emphasis we found prominent in the methodology of St. Anselm. Like Anselm, Barth warns against an anti-intellectualistic view of faith. "Without an increase of knowledge, there can be no increase in faith. . . ." [107] Finally, in order that faith be complete, it must become confession, that is, a witness to Jesus Christ who is acknowledged and known by man. [108]

The strict way in which Barth relates faith and knowledge should not be interpreted to mean that he equates faith with assent to doctrines or theological systems. Here Barth speaks of his negative agreement with Herrmann, Bultmann, and the existentialists who oppose such a view of faith. [109] For Barth faith is first and foremost the acknowledgment of "the One whom the Bible attests and the Church as taught by the Bible proclaims, the living Jesus Christ Himself, none other." [110] This rules out conceiving of faith as an independent act of man by means of which he merits salvation. With the Reformers, Barth contends that salvation by faith alone means that man acknowledges and trusts not in what he does for himself, but in what has been done for him in Jesus Christ. [111]

Barth's Critique of Natural Theology, Analogy, and Religion

Our discussion of Barth's doctrine of revelation has shown that he grounds both the objective and subjective reality and possibility of revelation in God. Our knowledge of God not only originates in his saving work in Jesus Christ but is also fulfilled through his work as Holy Spirit. Hence at the beginning as well as at the end of our knowledge of God, we must acknowledge with gratitude God's gracious self-manifestation in his revelation. Barth is quite aware of the circular nature of his argument in discussing revelation, but this is not due to a hidden metaphysic: it is due to the fact that God is both the origin and fulfiller of all human knowledge of him. The fact that this is said, however, does not assure that man's thought enters the circle of God's truth. In the final analysis, the theologian must acknowledge that it is only through grace that his knowledge participates in the truth of God. Thus in his reliance upon God's grace, man confesses that his knowledge can participate in the truth of God only through Jesus Christ and the work of his Spirit who are responsible both for its existence and its consummation.[112]

BARTH VS. NATURAL THEOLOGY

One of the points at which Anglo-Saxon theologians have been most critical of Barth is with respect to his consistent repudiation of natural theology and therewith his seemingly wholly negative estimate of God's revelation of himself in creation and man. This analysis of Barth's position is quite accurate: indeed, in his Gifford Lectures in the years 1937– 38, Barth referred to himself as an "avowed opponent of all natural theology."[113] However, in order to understand Barth's critique of natural theology, as well as his opposition to Catholic and Protestant use of the possibility of establishing a knowledge of God on the basis of the being common to both (*analogia entis*), and finally, his critique of man's "religion" as the pathway to knowledge of God, one must remember that they all derive from his developing christocentric doctrine of revelation.

All of these approaches to the knowledge of God are variants of what we designated "anthropological theology" at the outset of this chapter. This means that in Barth's view they speak about a knowledge of God which is possible on the basis of a universal revelation (general revelation) in creation, human history, or in the human consciousness. In his exposition of Romans, in the German church struggle, in his heated debate with Emil Brunner in 1934, and at different points in the *Church Dogmatics*, Barth develops an attack on natural theology which is without parallel in modern theology.

Barth recognizes that natural theology has played a prominent role in the history of the church from post-apostolic times to the present. Since the Middle Ages, Roman Catholicism has accepted and utilized a natural theology which establishes its knowledge of God, the Creator, on the basis of man's capacity as a rational being to interpret the revelation of God in nature, history, and in the human consciousness. According to Catholic dogma, this preliminary knowledge of God as Creator is supplemented by the truths about God which derive from the supernatural revelation of God attested in the Bible and interpreted by the Church. Though the Protestant Reformers made an occasional "unguarded" use of natural theology, Barth does not view them as advocates of natural theology. However, Protestant Orthodoxy did make use of natural theology and prepared the way for its inrush and importance in Protestant theology following the Enlightenment. As a consequence, Barth interprets Protestant theology of the last two hundred years in terms of repeated attempts to synthesize nature and grace. It tried to join a theology based on revelation in creation with a theology derived from God's redemptive activity in Israel and the church with its focus in Jesus Christ.[114]

The years of the German church struggle solidified Barth's attitude toward natural theology. He stood staunchly opposed to the German Christians who advocated a synthesis of German National Socialism as a second source of revelation with the gospel. In his estimate, this pernicious synthesis was not different in kind from others developed in neo-Protestantism. All detracted from the central revelation in Jesus Christ. This accounts for Barth's heated "No!" against Brunner in 1934.

In his *Nein* to Brunner, he wrote:

> Ever since about 1916, when I began to recover noticeably
> from the effects of my theological studies and the influences
> of the liberal-political pre-war theology, my opinion con-
> cerning the task of our theological generation has been this:
> we must learn again to understand revelation as *grace,* and
> grace as *revelation,* and therefore turn away from all "true"
> or "false" *theologia naturalis.*[115]

In the midst of the German church struggle concerning
the pathway to true knowledge of God, the Confessional
Church—which arose in opposition to the' Nazis and the
"German Christians"—met in 1934 in Barmen, Germany.
Barth's influence is evident throughout the Barmen Declaration and nowhere more than in its first article which affirms
that Jesus Christ is the "one Word of God," and thus the
sole means of all true knowledge of God. Hence the Confessional Church asserted: "We condemn the false doctrine that
the Church can and must recognize as God's revelation other
events and powers, forms and truths, apart from and along-
side this one Word of God."[116] Because of this unequivocal
stand with respect to the exclusiveness of the revelation of
God in Jesus Christ, Barth could describe the Barmen Declaration as the first repudiation of natural theology by the
Evangelical Church, and therefore "one of the most notable
events in modern Church History."[117]

We must conclude our discussion of Barth's attitude toward natural theology by looking at his definition of it and
by noting several reasons why he regards it as an "impossible" procedure.

> Natural theology is the doctrine of a union of man with God
> existing outside God's revelation in Jesus Christ. It works out
> the knowledge of God that is possible and real on the basis
> of this independent union with God, and its consequences
> for the whole relationship of God, world and man.[118]

In the first place, our analysis of Barth's doctrine of revelation has made it clear that for him all true knowledge of God is inextricably tied to God's self-revelation in Jesus Christ, which is made knowable through God's presence in his Spirit, and affirmed in faith. This rules out the possibility of arriving at a true knowledge of God which by-passes God's redemptive activity. It is therefore illegitimate to speak, as does natural theology, of a true knowledge of God the Creator which is divorced from a knowledge of God as Redeemer.

A second major reason why Barth opposes natural theology is that it cannot be justified on the basis of the biblical evidence. The main line of the scriptural witness is that the true knowledge of God—as Barth has shown—derives from God's special and redemptive activity within the history of the people of God in the old and new covenants. He admits that there are passages on the sideline or periphery of the Bible which affirm that both the created order and man reflect and confirm God's handiwork; he insists, however, that passages on the sideline must be interpreted as part of the single witness of the Bible to "God's revelation in Israel and in Jesus Christ." [119] These passages ought never to be interpreted as though man in the cosmos—without reference to God's revelation of himself—could arrive independently at a knowledge of God.[120] Whether the advocates of natural theology understood their procedure in the manner in which Barth portrays it is a question which we cannot consider here.

A third argument against natural theology is closely related to the foregoing. Barth emphasizes that the Bible views man as a sinner estranged from God and under divine judgment. There is no independent relationship to God or knowledge of God unaffected by man's sin. Paul's statement in Romans 3:22-24 underlines the universality of sin: "For there is no distinction; since all have sinned and fall short of the glory of God, they are justified by his grace as a gift, through the redemption which is in Christ Jesus" (RSV). Barth regards this affirmation to be representative of the main line of the Bible. Therefore, he warns against interpreting scattered references on the sideline in such a way as to accord man a knowledge of God which overlooks his sinfulness. Barth does not find the contention of the proponents of natural theology—that the natural man is both ready for, and open to, God's revelation—confirmed in the Scriptures. Precisely, the opposite is true. Man as such is the enemy of grace.[121]

The final and decisive reason why the Christian theologian must turn his back on natural theology is based on the fact that Jesus Christ is the one through whom men are reconciled to God. Jesus Christ is the man who is truly ready for, and open to, God. Hence the "knowability of God is not . . . to be made intelligible as the predicate of man as such."[122] It is through Jesus Christ and his perfect obedience on the cross that reconciliation between God and man is effected. Only by participating through faith in Jesus Christ as he is made known to us through his Spirit can man know God aright. Whenever the church and its proclamation is the captive of this revelation of God in Jesus Christ, it will regard natural theology as a fatal illusion. In this sphere man is concerned with his own "self-exposition and self-justification."[123]

Since man and his relationship to God is to be seen in the light of Jesus Christ, the attempt of natural theology to speak of man independently of him always represents a gross distortion.[124] The rigorous way in which Barth views human existence in the light of Jesus Christ alone accounts, in part, for his dissatisfaction with the attempts of Tillich and Bultmann to interpret man's understanding of his existence prior to his response of faith as a kind of prelude to faith, or at least as an indication of man's openness to God's grace.

THE ANALOGY OF FAITH VS. THE ANALOGY OF BEING

Since Barth's critique of natural theology is of a piece with his critique of the use of the analogy of being by Roman Catholics and others, we may deal with the latter very briefly.[125] The doctrine of the knowledge of God based on the analogy of being (*analogia entis*) affirms that since man and God share a like "being," man can arrive at some knowledge of God's being even apart from God's acts. Such an approach, like that of the natural theology based upon it, is deficient at several points. First, it divides the knowledge of God as Creator from knowledge of him as Redeemer. Second, it equates the highest being of man's projections with the biblical God. Third, it speaks of a knowledge of God apart from his acts. This contradicts an essential thrust of Barth's doctrine of God, namely, that God is who he is and is known as he is in the light of his acts alone.[126] In short, for Barth the natural knowledge of God based upon the analogy of being represents an abstraction and points to a woefully deficient understanding of God and of the nature of revelation.

In his doctrine of revelation, Barth opposes the analogy of being with the analogy of faith (*analogia fidei*). Knowledge of God is not obtainable on the basis of arguments reasoning from the being common to both man and God, but solely on the basis of God's grace known through faith. Man's language can point to God; in faith it may become true language about God. For Barth, however, this is always the sign of God's grace; it is never due to some capacity inherent in man or his language. To say, therefore, that our language is analogous to its object is to attest to God's sanctification of the views and concepts we use to refer to him. The fact that this occurs makes preaching and theology possible and is the foundation for all of man's knowledge of God.[127] When through the miracle of the Spirit's presence faith is awakened, the incongruity between man and God, between the knower and the known, is overcome; this event ought always to elicit man's joyful gratitude and reverent awe.[128]

BARTH VS. RELIGION

Since Barth's attitude towards the phenomenon of religion parallels in all essentials the critique of natural theology, a very brief statement of his provocative position must suffice.

Barth's analysis of the phenomenon of religion seeks to reverse the procedure which began in the Renaissance and culminated in neo-Protestantism. In it the biblical revelation was subordinated to the supposedly more comprehensive and universal category of religion.[129] Religion, like natural theology, must be judged and evaluated in the light of the biblical revelation. Since both the objective manifestation of God and man's subjective appropriation of his presence are the work of God, man's religion cannot be interpreted to accord him a capacity or some other possibility for knowing God. This is why Barth entitles his treatment of the problem of religion thus: "The Revelation of God as the Abolition of Religion."[130] Judged in the light of revelation, "Religion is unbelief. It is the one great concern . . . of godless man."[131]

It is important to note here that since the time that he wrote his *Romans*, Barth has been the foe of religion understood as the product of man's attempt to reach God on his own. Thus defined, religion is synonymous with the attempt of man to justify and save himself. In short, man's religion is always idolatry. On this account, Barth opposes the influential practice in modern Christian mission strategy of regarding other religions as a point of contact for the gospel. He does so for the same reasons he will not allow man's natural knowledge of God (natural theology) to be regarded as a level preliminary to Christian faith and therefore something with which Christian faith can be coordinated.

> Revelation does not link up with a human religion which is already present and practiced. It contradicts it, just as religion previously contradicted revelation. It displaces it, just as religion previously displaced revelation; just as faith cannot link up with a mistaken faith, but must contradict and displace it as unbelief, as an act of contradiction.[132]

Barth speaks of true religion as follows: "The Church is the locus of true religion, so far as through grace it lives by grace."[133] Thus not even the Christian religion is true in and of itself; in so far as the Christian religion represents the work of man, it is false religion and stands under the divine judgment. Even as the sinner stands in need of God's justification to be redeemed, so the Christian religion must be "exalted" into the true religion through God's grace.[134] To the extent that there are children of God in the church who live in reliance upon the grace of God in Jesus Christ, Barth must say that the Christian religion "alone is the true religion." [135]

III. Karl Barth's
Christocentric Theology

In this chapter our task is to illustrate how the centrality of God's revelation in Jesus Christ determines both the structure and content of various doctrines in the *Church Dogmatics*. Since space precludes surveying Barth's christocentrism completely, we must limit our attention to five major areas. First, brief mention must be made of his understanding of the "Reality of God" in terms of "The Being of God as the One who Loves in Freedom" (C.D. II/1). Second, we will pursue the doctrine of God further in giving special attention to Barth's doctrine of "The Election of God" (C.D. II/2). Third, Barth's approach to the doctrine of creation, especially his conception of the relationship of creation and covenant (C.D. III/1), will be indicated. Fourth, we will look at Barth's anthropology (C.D. III/2). Finally the main lines of the doctrine of reconciliation will be analyzed (C.D. IV/1–IV/3).

THE REALITY OF GOD: THE BEING OF GOD AS
THE ONE WHO LOVES IN FREEDOM

In discussing Barth's doctrine of revelation in the last chapter, we drew upon the first major division of his doctrine of God, which is entitled "The Knowledge of God" (C.D. II/1, chap. V). The next major division, "The Reality of God," is an exposition of "The Being of God as the One Who Loves in Freedom" (C.D. II/1, chap. VI). The being of the

living God is seen as love in his revelation in the Son through
which he establishes "fellowship between Himself and us,
and therefore He loves us."[1] But apart from and prior to
God's manifestation of himself as the one who loves in freedom, Barth maintains—in keeping with his Trinitarianism
—that God is the loving God who is free within himself.

With this view of the being of God arrived at through the
interpretation of God's revelation—thereby avoiding abstract
and impersonal conceptions of God's being—Barth proceeds
to develop the doctrine of God in terms of the divine perfections.[2] He holds that theology speaks of multiple divine at-
tributes or perfections in order to reflect the richness of God's
being; this does not contradict his oneness. This parallels
Barth's insistence that the three modes of God's being do not
undermine his unity.

Barth considers first the perfections of the "Divine Loving"
and then those of the "Divine Freedom." He depicts the reality
of God as love in terms of his perfections of grace and holiness, mercy and righteousness, and finally, patience and wisdom. The last perfection in each of these pairs accentuates
that the God who loves is the God who is free. Barth summarizes this section as follows:

> The divinity of the love of God consists and confirms itself
> in the fact that in Himself and in all His works God is gra-
> cious, merciful and patient, and at the same time holy, right-
> eous and wise.[3]

Barth analyzes the perfections of the divine freedom in
terms of God's oneness and omnipresence, constancy and
omnipotence, and finally eternity and glory. The first of
each of these pairs of perfections accentuates that God who
is free is one, constant, and eternal in himself and in all of
his works. The second points to the manner in which God is
free, namely, as omnipresent, omnipotent, and glorious. The
latter perfections reveal that God's "freedom is the freedom
of His love." [4] By proceeding thus, Barth develops his essen-

tial thesis that God is the being who loves in freedom.

In this brief survey of Barth's doctrine of the nature of God, we have not done justice to the way in which Jesus Christ is determinative of every Christian affirmation regarding God. Yet it should be evident that the portrayal of God's being as the one who loves in freedom is necessitated because in his action as Father, Son, and Holy Spirit he reveals himself to be this kind of God.[5] Thus to know God truly is not possible through speculation—which always issues in abstract and impersonal views of God as ultimate being. We affirm who God is on the basis of the "place where God deals with us as Lord and Saviour, or not at all."[6] Thus Barth recalls that

> in our consideration of the divine perfections everything became clear and orderly when He, Jesus Christ, emerged as the perfect One, the fulness of God Himself, the love and freedom of God in which all the divine perfections are neither more nor less than God Himself.[7]

THE DOCTRINE OF ELECTION

With this understanding of God in mind, we can better understand Barth's doctrine of election. Here more than anywhere else in the *Church Dogmatics* the intensification of his christocentrism is evident. Balthasar's estimate of the significance of Barth's doctrine of election is accurate:

> Without a doubt, this volume [on election] is the most magnificent, most unified and most carefully formulated part of the entire system; it is composed with the greatest love and represents the heart of Barth's theology. . . .[8]

Concerning the importance of this doctrine for the whole of his theology, Barth himself could say:

> The doctrine of election is the basic witness to the fact that the gracious God is the beginning of all the ways and works

of God. It defines grace as the starting-point for all subsequent reflection and speech, the common denominator which
should never be forgotten in any statement which follows,
and which should, if possible, come to expression in some
way in every subsequent statement.[9]

The Orientation of the Doctrine

Whoever wishes to comprehend Barth's doctrine of election must give careful attention to his introductory statement
on "The Orientation of the Doctrine":

> The doctrine of election is the sum of the Gospel because of
> all words that can be said or heard it is the best: that God
> elects man; that God is for man too the One who loves in
> freedom. It is grounded in the knowledge of Jesus Christ
> because He is both the electing God and elected man in One.
> It is part of the doctrine of God because originally God's
> election of man is a predestination not merely of man but
> of Himself. Its function is to bear basic testimony to eternal,
> free and unchanging grace as the beginning of all the ways
> and works of God.[10]

Several points deserve notice in assessing Barth's view of
God's election.

(1) An adequate doctrine of God must go beyond a deline-
ation of the divine perfections which are essential to his nature by asking what attitude God has taken toward everything
outside of himself. "We cannot speak accurately or con-
fidently of the work of God unless first we see clearly that
the attitude which God has taken up, and by which His work
is determined, belongs to God Himself and cannot in any way
be isolated from Him." [11]

(2) The answer to this question is to be found in God's
decision in "primal history"—or in eternity—to be "for
man" in Jesus Christ. Once again, Barth gives priority to the
particular over the general. God's concrete decision within
the Godhead to elect man to life and salvation through his

Son is the basis for understanding both subsequent covenant history and God's relationship with his creation, history, and all other men.[12] This explains why Barth can say that all "Christian truth" and "Christian doctrine" must necessarily reflect "this divine electing." Since this is so, the "doctrine of election occupies a place at the head of all other Christian dogmas. And it belongs to the doctrine of God Himself because God Himself does not will to be God, and is not God, except as the One who elects."[13]

(3) The fact that God elects to be God in this way underlines that he acts in sovereignty, freedom, and love. All of this is summed up by saying that God's election manifests his grace. Therefore the "function [of the doctrine of election] is to bear basic testimony to eternal, free and unchanging grace as the beginning of all the ways and works of God."[14]

(4) Because God elects man for salvation through Jesus Christ, Barth never tires of regarding the doctrine of election as the "sum of the Gospel." In this way he dispels the common notion that predestination is a gloomy doctrine. This attitude obtains because classical doctrines of election from Augustine to Aquinas and Calvin did not make clear that God's "yes" and his "no"—election to salvation or to reprobation—are not on the same level. The basic truth of God's election is the divine "yes," i.e., that "God so loved the world, that he gave his only begotten Son" (John 3:16).[15]

(5) In agreement with elements common to the classical doctrines of election, Barth also wants to affirm that this doctrine underscores the divine freedom. Since man is always the sinner met by God's free grace in Jesus Christ who was destined for his salvation from eternity, no possibility exists for man to merit salvation in any way. Man's only proper response to God's election through Jesus Christ is the grateful acceptance of his gift. Furthermore, to acknowledge God's election means to confess the mystery of election. Thus God's determination precedes man's self-determination.

(6) Finally, with earlier statements of predestination, Barth holds that God's election is righteous. As we shall see,

God's righteousness effects man's salvation—not his damnation. It is a merciful righteousness.[16]

The Foundation of the Doctrine

For Barth, the doctrine of election, like every other Christian doctrine, must have a biblical basis. This necessitates rejecting other approaches which might receive consideration. The theologian cannot presuppose some ecclesiastical doctrine of election as the correct one. This fact led Barth to remark in the preface to the volume on election: "I would have preferred to follow Calvin's doctrine of predestination more closely, instead of departing from it so radically. . . . but I could not and cannot do so. As I let the Bible itself speak to me on these matters, as I meditated upon what I seemed to hear, I was driven irresistibly to reconstruction."[17] Nor will Barth allow the pedagogical or pastoral utility of this doctrine to determine its content. Furthermore, he warns against the more serious error of constructing the doctrine of election on the basis of empirical observation of varied human responses to the gospel prior to listening to the Bible's testimony. Barth also rejects establishing what God's election means by investigating man's subjective experiences. Finally, attempts to establish the doctrine of election by beginning with a view of God as "omnipotent will," "irresistible omnipotence," "absolute World-ruler," or related conceptions, are to be rejected because they represent abstractions from the biblical understanding of God. "Theology must begin [in speaking about God] with Jesus Christ, and not with general principles. . . . Theology must also end with Him, and not with supposedly self-evident general conclusions . . . ."[18] This leads Barth to say: "As we have to do with Jesus Christ, we have to do with the electing God."[19] Any and all conceptions of what election means which are set forth without reference to Jesus Christ will be wide of the mark.[20]

The Election of Jesus Christ

The crucial paragraph summarizing Barth's christocentric

doctrine of election is found at the beginning of his section "The Election of Jesus Christ":

> The election of grace is the eternal beginning of all the ways and works of God in Jesus Christ. In Jesus Christ God in His free grace determines Himself for sinful man and sinful man for Himself. He therefore takes upon Himself the rejection of man with all its consequences, and elects man to participation in His own glory.[21]

On the basis of his exegesis of John 1:1-2, Ephesians 1:4ff., and other relevant New Testament passages,[22] Barth develops the doctrine of election. His concern is to show that Jesus Christ is eternally one with God in the unity of the Godhead. Therefore, it is not allowable to discuss God's electing will apart from Jesus Christ who is one with God from eternity. At the outset, Barth declares:

> It is by Him, Jesus Christ, and for Him and to Him, that the universe is created as a theatre for God's dealings with man and man's dealings with God. The being of God is His being, and similarly the being of man is originally His being. And there is nothing that is not from Him and by Him and to Him. He is the Word of God in whose truth everything is disclosed and whose truth cannot be over-reached or conditioned by any other word.[23]

This leads us to the heart of Barth's view of election. In essence, election refers to the decision of the triune God to effect his saving purpose in the world through his Word, the eternal Son of God.

> . . . Jesus Christ is Himself the divine election of grace. For this reason He is God's Word, God's decree and God's beginning. He is so all-inclusively, comprehending absolutely within Himself all things and everything, enclosing within Himself the autonomy of all other words, decrees and beginnings.[24]

That God's election must be referred to Jesus Christ is to be understood in a twofold sense. First, as true *God*, Jesus Christ is the subject who elects. Secondly, Jesus is also true *man*. As such, he is the elected man through whom other men are elected. Thus Jesus Christ is the object of God's election as well as the subject who elects. We must look at the meaning of Barth's views of election in terms of these two theses.

JESUS CHRIST, THE ELECTING GOD

The most surprising aspect of Barth's doctrine of election and the point at which he departs from the entire history of the doctrine of election is to be seen in the rigorous way in which he refuses to speak of God's decree of election apart from Jesus Christ. It is not sufficient to speak of Jesus Christ as the mirror or manifestation of God's electing will. This has been said often in the history of this doctrine. The crucial point is that in the sphere of primal history before creation Jesus Christ was *very God*; i.e., he was the active subject of election in his oneness with the Father and the Holy Spirit. Furthermore, Barth can say that the decree of election, in which the eternal Son participates, consists in the fact that in "an act of unconditional self-determination" God "ordained Himself as the bearer" of the name, Jesus Christ.[25] Thus "God anticipated and determined within Himself . . . that the goal and meaning of all His dealings with the as yet non-existent universe should be the fact that in His Son He would be gracious towards man, uniting Himself with him."[26]

Thus instead of positing an unknown, dark, and absolute decree as the origin of God's predestinating will, we must speak about Jesus Christ as the electing God and as the content of the divine election. Jesus Christ is God's concrete decree. Barth can say: "In its simplest and most comprehensive form the dogma of predestination consists, then, in the assertion that the divine predestination is the election of Jesus Christ."[27] The primal decree of God to be God *for man* in Jesus Christ governs all of his relationships to man in creation, reconciliation, and redemption. That the Father in union with the Son and the Spirit made this decision for the benefit of mankind enables Barth to affirm that the "election of grace is the eternal beginning of all the ways and works of God in Jesus Christ."[28] When Jesus Christ is seen as the electing God, the fatal error of Calvin and others, who separated the electing God from Jesus Christ, is avoided. To be sure, Calvin and Luther saw Jesus as the head of the elect. But neither related the revealed God in Jesus Christ and the hidden God to one another rigorously enough. For them the decree of predestination is dark and foreboding because it always referred to some decree apart from, and behind, Jesus Christ.

By viewing Jesus Christ as the electing God in this manner, Barth has made a move of decisive significance for his theology and the way in which all of God's dealing with man will be understood. The fact that Jesus Christ is the electing God and that we are elected by him and in him provides a certainty concerning our election which would be unobtainable on any other grounds. Barth concludes:

> . . . Jesus Christ reveals to us our election as an election which is made by Him, by His will which is also the will of God. He tells us that He Himself is the One who elects us. In the very foreground of our existence in history we can and should cleave wholly and with full assurance to Him because in the eternal background of history, in the beginning with God, the only decree which was passed, the only Word which was spoken and which prevails, was the decision which was executed by Him. As we believe in Him and hear His Word and hold fast by His decision, we can know with a certainty which nothing can ever shake that we are the elect of God.[29]

JESUS CHRIST, THE ELECTED MAN

We are now ready to look at the second major thesis of Barth's doctrine of election. It can be put simply. "Jesus Christ is the elected man."[30] Thus Jesus Christ is not only, as we have seen, the electing God, but is also the *object* of election. In "the beginning it was the choice of the Son to be

obedient to grace, and therefore to offer Himself and to become man in order that this covenant might be made a
reality." [31] Therefore, in speaking about who is elected, Barth
contends that

> the eternal divine decision as such has as its object and con-
> tent the existence of this one created being, the man Jesus
> of Nazareth, and the work of this man in His life and death,
> His humiliation and exaltation, His obedience and merit.
> It [this second thesis] tells us further that in and with the
> existence of this man the eternal divine decision has as its
> object and content the execution of the divine covenant with
> man, the salvation of all men. In this function this man is
> the object of the eternal divine decision and foreordination.
> Jesus Christ, then, is not merely one of the elect, but *the*
> elect of God. [32]

On the basis of Ephesians 1:4, Barth maintains that we are
elected only "in" Jesus Christ. He is the elected man. All other
men are elected because God foreordained their election
through the humanity of his Son.

> His election is the original and all-inclusive election; the
> election which is absolutely unique, but which in this very
> uniqueness is universally meaningful and efficacious, be-
> cause it is the election of Him who Himself elects. Of none
> other of the elect can it be said that his election carries in it
> and with it the election of the rest. [33]

From this perspective, Barth agrees with others who taught
that Jesus Christ is the mirror of what predestination always
means, namely, God's acceptance of man through his free
grace alone. The fact that the man Jesus is the head of the
elect is due to God's grace; so also is our inclusion in his
church. In looking at Jesus as the elected man we see that
God's purpose for man is that he be exalted to fellowship with
God. However, Jesus does more than simply reveal God's
intention for humanity at this point. For "God decreed too

that this man should be the cause and the instrument of our exaltation." [34]

Barth's purpose in viewing Jesus Christ both as the electing God and the elected man is to dispel the obscurity which has characterized doctrines of election at the point of identifying both the God who elects (or his decree) and the elect. Ordinarily, both were treated as unknown quantities. Hence the entire doctrine tended to be an enigma wrapped in a mystery. Barth contends that traditional statements saw Jesus Christ as the central point in God's redemptive work, but failed to correlate adequately what God did in Jesus Christ with God's eternal purpose. When speaking about God's eternal decree, they turned away from Jesus Christ, the revealed Word. Barth's question concerning this approach is: why should we refuse to look to Jesus Christ when dealing with predestination and God's foreordination of all things? If Jesus Christ is the same "yesterday, today and forever" (Heb. 13:8), we cannot think of God's will before creation apart from Jesus Christ any more than we think of the consummation apart from him. Therefore, in dealing with the electing God and the elected man, we are concerned with "only one name and one person, the same name and the same person, Jesus Christ." [35] This is the heart of the christocentric doctrine of election which Barth felt it necessary to develop on the basis of the biblical witness and because he could no longer accept the hiatus between christology and predestination in traditional doctrines of predestination. [36]

In an important paragraph, Barth summarizes the argument which we have developed thus far:

> The eternal will of God in the election of Jesus Christ is His will to give Himself for the sake of man as created by Him and fallen from Him. According to the Bible this was what took place in the incarnation of the Son of God, in His death and passion, in His resurrection from the dead. We must think of this as the content of the eternal divine predestination. The election of grace in the beginning of all things is

God's self-giving in His eternal purpose. His self-giving: God gave—not only as an actual event but as something eternally foreordained—God gave His only begotten Son. God sent forth His own Word. And in so doing He gave Himself. He gave Himself up. He hazarded Himself. He did not do this for nothing, but for man as created by Him and fallen away from Him. This is God's eternal will.[37]

DOUBLE PREDESTINATION

We take a final step in asking what Barth means by speaking of double predestination. In the first place, he emphasizes that God's eternal election is twofold in nature. On the one hand, it concerns the electing God; on the other, the elected man. God's electing will is twofold in the further sense (1) that God has predestined that he would have fellowship with man, and (2) that man would have fellowship with himself. The fact that predestination is twofold in the latter sense means "that God wills to lose in order that man may gain. There is a sure and certain salvation for man, and a sure and certain risk for God."[38]

This leads us to Barth's distinctive way of relating the concept of double predestination characteristic of the history of this doctrine to the election of Jesus Christ. In its simplest form this means (1) that God elected himself for suffering, rejection, death, and damnation, but (2) sinful man for salvation, blessedness, and eternal life. Let us survey each of these and the manner in which Barth relates this double predestination to Jesus Christ.

Let us look first at the negative pole of God's election. Here we are asking what it meant for God to elect to become man in the person of Jesus. It means that from all eternity God foreordained suffering and death for his Son. Jesus Christ is the "Lamb slain from the foundation of the world." The Son's self-emptying of which Paul speaks in Philippians 2:6ff. involved his obedience unto death on a cross. God in Jesus Christ took upon himself the rejection which rightfully belonged to sinful humanity. In his love God willed from eternity that in his Son he would take upon himself the judgment, rejection, death, and wrath which was man's lot as a consequence of his sin. "God from all eternity ordains this obedient One [Jesus Christ] in order that He might bear the suffering which the disobedient have deserved and which for the sake of God's righteousness must necessarily be borne." [39]

The rejection which the Son of God bore is thus one side of God's double decree. Barth pictures God as the "Eternal Judge" who allows himself to be judged in Jesus, thereby rescuing man from bondage to the satanic power. In so doing, God is true to his divine purpose and electing will. He does not spare his Son from suffering and death. Moreover, God raised Jesus from the dead thereby vindicating his purpose and overcoming Satan's power. It must also be said that throughout his life, Jesus is steadfast in his obedience to God. He does the will of his Father even unto death. Thus Barth can say: "In this twofold steadfastness there is to be seen both the glorifying of God and also the salvation of men, the two things which together constitute the aim and meaning of the covenant willed by God and the election of this man." [40]

This leads us to the positive pole of the election of God in Jesus Christ. That God in Jesus Christ elects man means that he foreordained man to live with him in the fellowship of the covenant. God in his Son bore rejection in order that man might enjoy salvation and eternal life. This explains why the message of election is the sum of the gospel and therefore good news.

Even though man lives his life in the midst of threatening powers of evil, he has assurance on the basis of God's electing love in Jesus Christ that God's final purpose cannot be overcome. Therefore, Barth opposes the traditional doctrines of predestination which teach that God's intention for man might just as well be reprobation and condemnation as election to life and blessedness. To be sure, the power of evil continues to exist within the divine permission, but man is not predestined to be overcome by it. He is foreordained to life and participation in the glory of God. Therefore, God's electing will is not a mixture of joy and terror, light and darkness. On account of God's electing love in Jesus Christ, man's destiny is eternal life—never death. That this is God's will for mankind is attested in the fact that God raised his Son from the dead.[41] Thus Barth regards God's electing decree, actualized in the history of salvation and supremely in Jesus Christ, as the key to understanding the history of the world as well.[42]

JESUS CHRIST, THE ELECTED COMMUNITY, THE ELECTED INDIVIDUAL

A brief statement must suffice concerning the manner in which God's eternal decree becomes effective in history. Again, Barth's approach is somewhat distinctive. The biblical order to be followed in speaking about election is: (1) Jesus Christ, the Elector and Elected; (2) the Elect Community, Israel and the church, and (3) finally, the elect individual. First and always, everything which is said about God's election must have reference to Jesus Christ. However, Barth rejects the prevalent tendency to move immediately from God's electing love in Jesus Christ to the question of the individual's election. He devotes an entire section to God's election of the community or people of God before discussing the election of the individual (C.D. II/2, par. 34-35). The one community of God which exists in a twofold form, namely as Israel and the church, has for its purpose to witness to Jesus Christ in the world and to "summon the whole world to faith in Him." It is in a "mediate" position between Jesus Christ and those individuals who through his election will become believers; thus the relation between the election of Jesus Christ and all individual believers is "mediated and conditioned by" the community. Therefore, Barth affirms with the ancient church: "outside the Church, there is no salvation."[43]

The one community which is included in the election of Jesus Christ has a twofold form which corresponds to the twofold predestination evident in the election of Jesus Christ. "Jesus Christ is the crucified Messiah of Israel. As such He is the authentic witness of the judgment that God takes upon

Himself by choosing fellowship with man."⁴⁴ Israel stands
as a sign of the people of God who again and again disobey
God, and thus points to the necessity of the divine judgment.
Israel attests the judgment and the negative side of election
which was borne by their Messiah. However, on the basis of
Romans 9–11, Barth argues that Israel's ultimate destiny is
to believe on Jesus Christ and therefore no longer to be a sign
of the people who fail to believe in their election.

The same Jesus Christ is "also the risen Lord of the
Church." If Israel is the sign of the old man, the church is the
sign of the new humanity begun in Jesus Christ. The church
attests the positive side of God's electing love for man manifest in Jesus Christ; it exists to point the world to God's
mercy, love, and grace attested supremely in Jesus' resurrection from the dead. Barth summarizes the mission of the
church in the world as follows:

> The Church thus proclaims Jesus' exaltation as the goal of
> His humiliation, His kingdom as the goal of His suffering,
> His coming as the goal of His passing. It proclaims what in
> God's hands is to become and can become of man taken up
> and accepted by Him.⁴⁵

Finally, Barth deals with the individual's election which
can be understood only in the light of the election of Jesus
Christ and the community elected through him. The election
of individuals is the real goal of the election of the community. However, individuals are not elected on the basis of their
individuality or because of some merit. Rather through the
work of the Holy Spirit, each acknowledges through faith his
election in Jesus Christ. The elect individual is, therefore,
one who has responded in faith to the Word of God spoken in
Jesus Christ.

It must be emphasized that Barth speaks of a special "determination of the elect." This means in essence that "an elect
man is in any case elect in and with and by and for Jesus

Christ." [46] His election involves participation in the ministry of the church. Here Barth stresses that the witness of the church and elect individuals must be the proclamation of the good news of God's love for man in Jesus Christ. Neither the church nor the individual believer is called to determine who the elect will be. Neither are called upon to declare that God wills man's damnation. In his summary thesis concerning the election of the individual, Barth affirms the positive note which should characterize the church's witness.

> The man who is isolated over against God is as such rejected by God. But to be this man can only be the godless man's own choice. The witness of the community of God to every individual man consists in this: that this choice of the godless man is void; that he belongs eternally to Jesus Christ and therefore is not rejected, but elected by God in Jesus Christ; that the rejection which he deserves on account of his perverse choice is borne and cancelled by Jesus Christ; and that he is appointed to eternal life with God on the basis of the righteous, divine decision. The promise of his election determines that as a member of the community he himself shall be a bearer of its witness to the whole world. And the revelation of his rejection can only determine him to believe in Jesus Christ as the One by whom it has been borne and cancelled. [47]

Such statements and the logic of Barth's entire doctrine of election have led numerous critics to charge Barth with teaching universal salvation. Barth is quite sensitive to this charge. However, he maintains that it does not fall within man's prerogative to determine the scope of God's election. In deference to the freedom of God's grace, we are precluded from denying the possibility of universal salvation in principle. In short, man cannot set limits to God's gracious activity. In the meantime, however, Barth's conception of the mission of the church and the Christian is clear: the gospel must be proclaimed in the hope that God's will is always to increase the

number of the elect. "It belongs to God Himself to determine
and to know what it means that God was reconciling the world
unto Himself (2 Cor. 5:19)."[48]

In conclusion, we must look with Barth at the "determination of the rejected." There are those who live as though they
were rejected of God, and there are those who do not believe
in their election unto salvation in Jesus Christ. What is God's
will for them? In order to understand Barth's position we
must remember the following: "The rejection of mankind is
the rejection borne eternally and therefore for all time by
Jesus Christ in the power of divine self-giving."[49] Therefore,
to live as though one were rejected of God is to live a lie.
However, the individual who lives in this way serves to
remind the believer—even as Israel reminds the church—of
the rejection which has, in fact, been carried by Jesus Christ.
Yet in the light of God's loving-kindness in Jesus Christ, the
message of the church to Israel and to individuals who live
as the "rejected" is to affirm in faith their election in Jesus
Christ.[50]

THE DOCTRINE OF CREATION

To this point we have given major attention to Barth's doctrine of God and particularly his view of God's eternal election of Jesus Christ as the foundation and goal of all of his
works. Now we must look at Barth's christological approach
to the doctrine of creation as the first of God's works. Conscious of critics who predicted that his critique of natural
theology would preclude his development of a doctrine of
creation, Barth unfolds this doctrine in a massive third volume composed of four parts. These deal successively with:
"The Work of Creation" (C.D. III/1); "The Creature" (C.D.
III/2); "The Creator and His Creature" (C.D. III/3); and
"The Command of God the Creator" (C.D. III/4).

Barth introduces the entire doctrine of creation with a
section entitled "Faith in God the Creator." He opposes constructing the doctrine of creation on the basis of insights

gained from God's universal revelation and a natural theology built thereon, or upon philosophical or scientific speculation about, or investigaton of, creation. Barth contends that knowledge of God as Creator and of his relationship to his creation and with man is certain only in so far as it derives from the biblical witness and supremely from the center of that witness, namely, Jesus Christ. Hence it is an article of faith to believe in God as Creator and in the reality of the world and of the creature he created. Barth can say: "It is here [i.e., in Jesus Christ] that God Himself has revealed the relationship between Creator and creature—its basis, norm and meaning." [51]

This view is in harmony with Barth's christological doctrine of election developed above. God's act of creation is the first of his works which from eternity are directed toward the realization of his saving purpose. The fact that the being of God as Creator and his work of creation cannot be understood apart from Jesus Christ is grounded in the fact that Christ as the eternal Word of God (John 1:1–3) is one with God from eternity and therefore shares in the act of creation. Thus, faith in Jesus Christ "contains within itself the knowledge of the secret of creation, the Creator and the creature." [52]

Barth's christocentrism also provides the basis for interpreting the twofold thesis he develops with respect to the relationship of creation and covenant within the will of God. The thesis is (1) that creation provides the external basis of God's covenant of grace with man and (2) that this covenant of grace is the internal basis of creation. [53]

In order to understand how Barth relates creation and covenant, we must recall the major thesis of his doctrine of election, namely, that from eternity God foreordained that he would become man in Jesus Christ in order to reconcile sinful man with himself. In order to effect his purpose, God engages in the first of his works—namely, creation—which provides the place in which he will institute, preserve, and execute the covenant of grace between himself and man. Thus "creation sets the stage for the story of the covenant of grace." [54] Barth justifies his view of "creation as the external basis of the covenant" in terms of his exegesis of the first creation narrative (Gen. 1:1–2:4a). In this emphasis Barth echoes Calvin's teaching that creation is the theater in which God reveals his glory.

The second major thesis Barth develops is derived from the second creation narrative (Gen. 2:4bff.). Here Barth finds the emphasis which enables him to speak of "the covenant as the internal basis of creation." In so doing, Barth accentuates the basic theme of his doctrine of election, namely, that all of God's dealings with man in creation are directed ultimately toward the fulfillment of his covenant of grace revealed in Jesus Christ. Therefore, although he treats the covenant as the internal basis of creation only in the second major division of his doctrine of creation and covenant, it is actually prior in significance (ontologically) to the first thesis. Creation precedes the beginning of the covenant in point of time, but the latter precedes and is the presupposition of creation within the divine purpose.

Barth expresses the manner in which the covenant history is the internal basis of creation by maintaining that the "history of salvation" is the "true history" which determines all other history. Everything which can be said about the relationships of God to man, creation, and history must derive from the history of salvation which makes his will and purpose known.[55] "The covenant of grace is *the* theme of history. The history of salvation is *the* history."[56] Barth summarizes the relationship of creation and covenant in asserting that, according to the Bible's witness,

> the purpose and therefore the meaning of creation is to make possible the history of God's covenant with man which has its beginning, its centre and its culmination in Jesus Christ. The history of this covenant is as much the goal of creation as creation itself is the beginning of this history.[57]

In the light of this understanding of creation, Barth is able to conclude his treatment of "The Work of Creation" by speaking of "The Yes of God the Creator." The existence and reality of creation and the creature are good as created, actualized, and justified by God. Through faith, man may respond to God's "yes" to him, thereby accepting his creatureliness, because God as Creator has affirmed man as his creature and ordained that through Jesus Christ he should live as his covenant-partner. Moreover, the fact that God rescued man from the threatening power of evil through the life, death, and resurrection of his Son is the basis for "Christian optimism."[58]

THE DOCTRINE OF MAN

Barth's anthropology is unfolded in Volume III/2 of the *Church Dogmatics*—a book over 600 pages in length! The special care he accorded this subject may be seen as a partial answer to those who prophesied that Barth, who in early writings stressed man's fall and sin, would never be able to develop an adequate doctrine of man. However, as early as 1932, Barth anticipated the direction which his anthropology was to take in saying: "There is a way from Christology to anthropology. There is no way from an anthropology to Christology."[59] Thus from the beginning of the *Church Dogmatics*, Barth's concern was a truly theological or christological anthropology.

With the publication of his anthropology in 1948, Barth maintains—as we have been led to expect—that "Man is made an object of theological knowledge by the fact that his relationship to God is revealed to us in the Word of God."[60] Nontheological anthropologies, whether of the speculative, philosophical type or of the nonspeculative, scientific type, may contribute to a technological understanding of man and the "phenomena of the human," but they cannot uncover man's true being. They may help in interpreting certain aspects of human existence, but their presuppositions preclude discovering the mystery of "real man." In order to know the mystery of human nature, we cannot begin with man's natural self-understanding. In agreement with Calvin, Barth affirms that true self-knowledge and the knowledge of God are correlates. Knowledge of man's true nature as the creature of God obtains only from listening to the Word of God revealed in Jesus Christ.[61]

Jesus, the Real Man

This brings us to the decisive statement which undergirds Barth's christological anthropology. "As the man Jesus is Himself the revealing Word of God, He is the source of our knowledge of the nature of man as created by God."[62] In adopting this position, Barth contends he has made an even more radical break with tradition than in his doctrine of election. The issue raised by this christological anthropology is not whether such an approach is possible, but whether it is "the only one possible."[63]

In order, therefore, to discover "real man," we do not look first of all at man, the sinner, but at "Jesus, the Man for God."[64] Barth's stand is unequivocal: "The ontological determination of humanity is grounded in the fact that one man among all others is the man Jesus."[65] What God intends human nature to be is revealed in the human nature of Jesus, the Second Adam, and not through an analysis of the first Adam. This does not mean that we can equate our human nature with that of Jesus, or that we can deduce anthropology directly from christology. Jesus expresses human nature perfectly whereas all other men do so imperfectly. He is different from us both on account of his unity with God and because he is without sin. Nevertheless, the fact that we share a common humanity with Jesus means that we may learn "indirectly" what constitutes human nature in general, by looking at his human nature.

Assuming hypothetically that Jesus is the only source of our knowledge of human nature, Barth finds the following characteristics of human nature suggested.

(1) ". . . among all creatures man, i.e., this man, is the

one in whose identity with himself we must recognize at once the identity of God with Himself." [66]

(2) God acts in this man. "His presence in Him means that the history of deliverance is enacted and His revelation in Him means that this history must be known." [67]

(3) God does not "lose himself" by being present in Jesus. He retains his sovereignty and deity. [68]

(4) Jesus is the real man because God is in him. Indeed, "this man is the imminent kingdom of God." [69]

(5) This man exists to do his Father's will. Therefore, what he is cannot be determined apart from his saving mission.

(6) Barth sums up the characteristics of the man, Jesus, in saying: "the distinctiveness of this creature consists in the fact that it is for God." [70]

How then are we to characterize human nature in light of the perfect human nature of Jesus?

It must be stressed first that "to be a man is to be with God." [71] Barth makes this basic assertion because the proper conception of human nature is to read from the nature of the man Jesus, who must be understood in the light of his relationship to God. [72] Jesus, the

> divine Counterpart of every man, of man as such, is concretely this one man in whose creaturely being we have to do with the existence, the saving act, the glory and lordship and the fulfillment of the will of God—with the creaturely being existing for God. [73]

As this particular being, Jesus manifests his divinity. For Barth, therefore, Jesus as the God-man reflects "the transcendence of God" uniquely and comprehensively. The human nature of all other men in "fellowship with Jesus" also reflects and represents the transcendence of God. Thus the "hidden being" of all creatures—the secret of human nature—is revealed in the man Jesus, and in his relationship to God. It follows that "man is with God because he is with

Jesus."[74] Since this is so, godlessness in no way is to be regarded as characteristic of the real man. "To be in sin, in godlessness, is a mode of being contrary to our humanity."[75]

Second, Barth amplifies the manner in which man's nature is always to be viewed in terms of his relationship to God by teaching that "the being of man as a being with Jesus rests upon the election of God. . . ."[76] Here Barth reiterates that Jesus is the elected man, and that all other men are elected in him. "To be a man is thus to be with the One who is the true and primary Elect of God."[77] This means that man is predestined in Jesus Christ to be delivered from the power of sin and nonbeing which contradict the divine will. Human nature is thus determined from all eternity and must be understood in this way in the light of the elected man, Jesus.[78]

A further related characteristic of man's true nature is "that it consists in the hearing of the Word of God."[79] That is to say, Jesus is the supreme Word of God. In him, we are confronted with the actualization of God's eternal will for his creatures. To be human means, therefore, "to be in the particular sphere of the created world in which the Word of God is spoken and sounded."[80] Therefore, man is the creature "addressed, called and summoned by God."[81] We cannot understand man's true nature if we abstract it from the "universal truth" that the Word of God in Jesus Christ determines what constitutes human nature. In this sense, Barth can speak of man being "in the Word of God."[82]

Fourth, Barth sums up the foregoing by stating that "the being of man is a history."[83] That this is the case is determined by the fact that "primal history" occurs as event when God, the Creator, became a creature in Jesus. Apart from Jesus' history, it would be possible to describe human existence simply in terms of a "state" of being. But the history of the man Jesus is the basis for interpreting man's existence as history. "Their being is history in or with the history enacted in the existence of the man Jesus."[84] Expressed differently, Barth is saying that because of the similarity between Jesus' humanity and that of all men, and because of

who he is, all other men are caught up in the history of salvation and redemption. Man's "true being is his being in the
history grounded in the man Jesus, in which God wills to be
for him and he may be for God." [85]

Up to this point we have observed that in the light of the
man Jesus, Barth interprets man's being as derived from God
and therefore as a "being with God." Moreover, it was noted
that human existence must be seen in terms of the divine election which, in turn, involves man's hearing the Word of God
which summons him in Jesus Christ. All in all, this means
that man's true being and existence is historical in the fullest
sense, as he participates in God's redemptive purpose effected
through Jesus.

Finally, Barth depicts "real man" as the creature confronted, maintained, and delivered through the grace of God
in Jesus Christ. Man's proper response to God's grace is gratitude. Thus the "being of man is a being in gratitude." [86] As
the recipient of God's grace, man is wholly receptive; in
responding with spontaneity and freedom to God's grace in
gratitude and thanksgiving, man actively realizes his destiny
as God's creature.

By living responsibly under God, man comes to know God
and himself, in that order. His existence is characterized by
"obedience to God" and the "invocation of God." He may
live making use of the "freedom with which he had been
endowed by God." [87] When man lives related to God in the
foregoing manner, he lives responsibly. For man to sin means
that he has "renounced his freedom"; he fails to live as the
good creature God created him to be. [88]

To this point, we have discussed only the first major section
of Barth's anthropology—"Man as the Creature of God." In
each of the three remaining sections, Barth deals first with
the man Jesus, and then with human nature in general. In
depicting "Man in his Determination as the Covenant-Partner
of God," Barth begins with a treatment of "Jesus, Man for
Other Men." In considering "Man as Soul and Body," we
confront first "Jesus, Whole Man." Finally, the treatment of

"Man in His Time" is introduced with a study of "Jesus,
Lord of Time." [89]

Man, the Covenant-Partner of God

The countless new and suggestive turns which Barth's
christological anthropology takes can only be hinted at in
this concluding statement. We have seen that the nature of
man cannot be understood apart from his creation by, and
relationship to, God. The existence of the real man and the
purpose of his life are illuminated further in Barth's treatment of man as "the covenant-partner of God." He summarizes the matter thus:

> That real man is determined by God for life with God has its
> inviolable correspondence in the fact that his creaturely be-
> ing is a being in encounter—between I and Thou, man and
> woman. It is human in this encounter, and in this humanity
> it is a likeness of the being of its Creator and a being in hope
> in Him. [90]

Barth's main thrust in this section is set forth in the thesis
that the essence of the humanity of Jesus of Nazareth is to be
seen in that he is "The Man" who lives wholly for his fellow-
man. Hence the humanity of Jesus "is to be described un-
equivocally as fellow-humanity." [91] To understand Jesus'
humanity is to see him as one whose mission—in keeping with
God's eternal intention—is to live for others as their deliverer
and Savior. Thus Barth can say:

> The humanity of Jesus is not merely the repetition and re-
> flection of His divinity, or of God's controlling will; it is the
> repetition and reflection of God Himself, no more and no
> less. It is the image of God, the *imago Dei*. [92]

If Jesus' cohumanity is the essential sign of his human
nature and the reflection of the primal truth that God is eternally "for" man, how does this relate to Barth's interpreta-

tion of human nature in general? First, it means that man is so created that he, too, is able to live in fellowship with God as his creaturely partner in the covenant. Despite the dissimilarity between man's sinful nature and Jesus' perfect human nature, a certain similarity still obtains. Second, Barth is able to "describe humanity as a being of man with others."[93] Therefore, Nietzsche was wrong in depicting true humanity as man without his fellow-man arrayed against the crucified Christ.

Man realizes what it means to be a human being to the extent that he lives for others and with others by entering into fellowship and dialogue with them. Every positive encounter between man and his neighbor, between I and Thou, reflects the truth that man is created for community. The basic form of this life of community is seen in the relationship of man to woman. Hence Barth speaks of Genesis 2:18–25—which tells of the creation of woman for man—as the "Magna Carta of humanity."[94] It follows that whenever man lives in the relationship of an I to a Thou, he is the image of God. As such, he reflects not only the essential truth that he is created for community, but also that God in his triune being is a communal being. Since to be in the image of God means to be created in this way, Barth contends that man does not cease being in the image of God because of his sin.[95]

None of these facts about man's true humanity can be known in their full significance apart from knowing God through faith. For Barth, man can neither know that he is a sinner nor that he is created in the image of God apart from faith in Jesus Christ. Thus the person of Jesus Christ is constitutive both for determining the basic structure of humanity (ontologically) and for our knowledge of it (noetically).

In conclusion, it can be said that Barth's christological anthropology breaks with all attempts in modern theology to construct a doctrine of man by beginning with man's self-knowledge divorced from revelation. Consequently, it represents the most consistent theological position in twentieth-

century theology, interpreting human nature by beginning
with the man Jesus, rather than with a phenomenological
analysis of human existence in general.

THE DOCTRINE OF RECONCILIATION

Nowhere does Barth's magnification of the person and work
of Jesus Christ resound more fully than in his "Doctrine of
Reconciliation" developed in three large volumes plus a
fragment (C.D. IV/1, 1953; C.D. IV/2, 1955; C.D. IV/3-I
& II, 1959; (fragment) C.D. IV/4, 1967. His final creative
work was expressed in this four-part volume which concludes
the *Church Dogmatics.* Our survey of this crucial doctrine
must be brief. Since we cannot expound its full content, we
must focus upon the way in which the person of Jesus Christ
determines its structure.

The Subject and Its Problems

God's purpose to "reconcile the world" unto himself in
his Son—his eternal plan—is determinative for Barth's entire theology. We have seen its significance for interpreting
the nature of God; for viewing creation as the place ordained
for the establishment and enactment of God's covenant; for
understanding man as God's creature ordained to be his covenant-partner; for interpreting the history of the covenant
which begins with Israel and continues to the present in the
history of the church; and finally, for understanding the
manner in which the incarnation, life, death, and resurrection
of Jesus Christ and the continuation of his work through the
Holy Spirit effects reconciliation between sinful man and God
and thus fulfills the broken covenant between them.

Barth introduces the scope of the doctrine of reconciliation
as follows:

> The subject-matter, origin and content of the message re-
> ceived and proclaimed by the Christian community is at its
> heart the free act of the faithfulness of God in which He

takes the lost cause of man, who has denied Him as Creator and in so doing ruined himself as creature, and makes it His own in Jesus Christ, carrying it through to its goal and in that way maintaining and manifesting His own glory in the world.[96]

Man realizes the purpose which God has for him not on the basis of capacities which he retains as sinner, but through God's gracious and reconciling action in his behalf in Jesus Christ. He restores the covenant broken by sinful man. God's covenant with Israel is the presupposition of God's reconciling work in Jesus Christ; but at a deeper level, the Old Covenant was instituted for the purpose of effecting reconciliation between the whole of sinful humanity and God through Jesus Christ. The sin of humanity contradicts God's intention— it is contrary to the will of the Creator but does not represent an insuperable obstacle to his grace. In Jesus Christ, God humbles himself by becoming man, taking up man's "lost cause" by assuming the judgment for sin which rightfully belonged to man, thereby effecting reconciliation. Typical of Barth's entire treatment is his emphasis that the objective reality of man's reconciliation with God is effected wholly by Jesus Christ. However, though Barth speaks of all men being justified, sanctified, and called in and through what God in Jesus Christ has done once and for all, he also gives attention to man's subjective appropriation of reconciliation through the work of God as Holy Spirit. The Spirit effects the "gathering," "upbuilding," and mission of the church in the world. Through the Spirit's witness there are individuals who in faith accept justification through Jesus Christ, and who acknowledge their sanctification in Jesus Christ, receiving power through the Spirit to live in his service and in love. Finally, through the Spirit's enlightenment, individual Christians in their vocations are marked by hope as they look toward the future consummation of the kingdom of God through Jesus Christ.

We have surveyed something of the grandeur of Barth's

doctrine of reconciliation. A brief indication of the way in which Jesus Christ accomplishes man's reconciliation with God and is determinative for the content and structure of this doctrine must suffice. First, Barth views Jesus Christ as the *true God* who humbles himself as a servant and in so doing is the reconciling God. This is the priestly work of Jesus Christ which accomplishes man's justification (C.D. IV/1). Second, Jesus Christ is *true man,* i.e., he is the servant or Son of Man who is exalted by God and is therefore the reconciled man through whom all others are exalted to fellowship with God (C.D. IV/2). This is Christ's kingly work which effects man's sanctification. Finally, Jesus Christ as the Mediator of man's reconciliation with God is the *God-man;* as such, he is the "guarantor and witness" of our atonement effected through him. This is Christ's prophetic work through which he equips man for his calling as a witness to his reconciling work (C.D. IV/3-I & II).[97]

By adopting this approach, Barth makes it clear from the outset that Jesus Christ is the key to the entire doctrine of reconciliation. More precisely, the Mediator, Jesus Christ, "is the atonement as the fulfillment of the covenant."[98] The Mediator is the one in whom the reconciling God and the reconciled man are both present. "He exists as the Mediator between God and man in the sense that in Him God's reconciling of man and man's reconciliation with God are event."[99] For this reason Barth sometimes can say that Jesus Christ himself is the event of reconciliation.[100] We must note also that Jesus Christ is not only the clue to interpreting God's reconciling work on its objective side. The believer's appropriation of what God in Christ has done for the world, through faith, love, and hope as these are called into being by the Holy Spirit, cannot be understood without constant reference to Jesus Christ. He is also the key for understanding the nature of man's sin. In this sense, Jesus Christ is the "beginning and the middle and the end" of the doctrine of reconciliation in all of its parts.[101]

Jesus Christ, the Lord as Servant

The first section of the doctrine of reconciliation Barth entitles "Jesus Christ, the Lord as Servant." The major thesis which he develops here under the caption, "The Obedience of the Son of God," deserves citation:

> That Jesus Christ is very God is shown in His way into the far country in which He the Lord became a servant. For in the majesty of the true God it happened that the eternal Son of the eternal Father became obedient by offering and humbling Himself to be the brother of man, to take His place with the transgressor, to judge him by judging Himself and dying in his place. But God the Father raised Him from the dead, and in so doing recognised and gave effect to His death and passion as a satisfaction made for us, as our conversion to God, and therefore as our redemption from death to life.[102]

Barth interprets the New Testament teaching concerning the condescension of God in his incarnate Son as "The Way of the Son of God into the Far Country."[103] In keeping with his Chalcedonian christology developed earlier in the *Church Dogmatics*, Barth insists that it is "very God" or the true God who is present in Jesus Christ. By becoming "very man" or true man, God did not cease being God. In Jesus Christ we are confronted by him who is truly God and truly man at the same time. It is precisely in God's condescension in his Son that his deity is revealed. We are therefore forbidden to speculate about God's deity apart from Jesus Christ. In the Son's incarnation, and in his obedience to his Father's will even unto death, we are confronted with the Lord who became a servant. God manifests his nature as the one who loves in freedom in his condescension in his Son. God is able to do this and he does it.

This leads us to ask how God in Jesus Christ effects man's salvation. In Barth's doctrine of election we saw the manner in which he stressed God's saving purpose from eternity.

Therefore, the fact that God became "the brother of man" in Jesus Christ is to be understood as the realization of his will to save his wayward creature and covenant-partner. God moves toward man in Jesus Christ because of his mercy and grace. God is "for us" in Jesus Christ; he identifies with sinners by being their brother. Concerning what this means concretely, Barth writes:

> *Deus pro nobis* [God for us] means simply that God has not abandoned the world and man in the unlimited need of his situation, but that He willed to bear this need as His own, that He took it upon Himself, and that he cries with man in this need.[104]

We must proceed a step further in describing the way in which God in Christ effects our deliverance and reconciliation. Jesus Christ comes as the Judge of the world and of all men because of who he is. The plight of sinful man is pictured by Barth as the perennial attempt to be "his own judge" and master of his own destiny. All men are guilty of this basic sin and therefore all stand under the divine sentence. But—and here we are met with the mystery of God's merciful judgment of man in Jesus Christ—God allowed his Son to be judged in our place. "What took place is that the Son of God fulfilled the righteous judgment on us men by Himself taking our place as man and in our place undergoing the judgment under which we had passed."[105]

It is essential at this point that we view the exchange which Christ effected quite literally. Barth affirms a radically substitutionary view of the atonement. He who is the Judge, the only one who is sinless, the one who alone is righteous, takes the sin of man upon himself. Jesus the Priest becomes the victim. This is the meaning of the rejection, suffering, and crucifixion which Jesus accepts in obedience to his Father's will. This is Barth's interpretation of the priestly work of Jesus Christ. He is our representative in that he took upon himself the judgment we deserved.

In His doing this for us, in His taking to Himself—to fulfill all righteousness—our accusation and condemnation and punishment, in His suffering in our place and for us, there came to pass our reconciliation with God. *Cur Deus Homo?* [Why did God become man?] In order that God as man might do and accomplish and achieve and complete all this for us wrong-doers, in order that in this way there might be brought about by Him our reconciliation with Him and conversion to Him.[106]

This brings us to the manner in which Barth interprets the resurrection of Jesus Christ as "The Verdict of the Father" through which God's saving purpose in the cross is vindicated. Here the "intensive, although for the most part quiet, debate with Rudolf Bultmann" of which Barth speaks in the preface is quite apparent.[107] Whereas Bultmann speaks only of the rise of the Easter faith in the disciples and refuses to speak of the resurrection as an event, separate from the cross, occurring in space and time, Barth insists that the "New Testament is speaking of an event in time and space."[108] The sovereign "yes" which God utters in raising Jesus Christ from the dead means further that the final word is not that "in his person, with Him, judgment, death and end have come to us ourselves once and for all."[109] The resurrection means positively that we are given room to live and trust in him who is the risen Lord. Barth puts the significance of the resurrection of Jesus from the dead as follows:

To sum up, the resurrection of Jesus Christ is the great verdict of God, the fulfillment and proclamation of God's decision concerning the event of the cross. It is its acceptance as the act of the Son of God appointed our representative, an act which fulfilled the divine wrath but did so in the service of the divine grace. It is its acceptance as the act of His obedience which judges the world, but judges it with the aim of saving it. It is its acceptance as the act of His Son whom He has always loved (and us in Him), whom of His sheer goodness He has not rejected but drawn to Himself (and us in

Him) (Jer. 31:3). In this the resurrection is the justification
of God Himself, of God the Father, Creator of heaven and
earth, who has willed and planned and ordered this event. It
is the justification of Jesus Christ, His Son, who willed to suf-
fer this event, and suffered it to the very last. And in His
person it is the justification of all sinful men, whose death
was decided in this event, for whose life there is therefore no
more place. In the resurrection of Jesus Christ His life and
with it their life has in fact become an event beyond death:
"Because I live, ye shall live also" (John 14:19).[110]

MAN, THE SINNER

Contrary to the traditional procedure in systematic theology according to which the doctrine of sin is developed prior
to the doctrine of reconciliation, Barth goes his own way once
again and opts for a christocentric starting point. At the outset of his anthropology, he said: "The doctrine of sin belongs
to the context of the doctrine of reconciliation."[111] Therefore,
Barth interprets the nature and consequences of man's sin
against the backdrop of each of the three main parts of the
doctrine of reconciliation.[112] Man's dilemma as sinner is
compounded because sin distorts his self-understanding with
respect to his relationship to God and the nature of his sin.
He may become aware of the ambiguities and tensions within
his existence, but he cannot recognize the gravity of his situation vis-à-vis God. "Access to the knowledge that he is a sinner is lacking to man because he is a sinner. We are presup-
posing agreement on this point. All serious theology has tried
to win its knowledge of sin from the Word of God and to base
it on that Word."[113] All of man's attempts to discover the
truth about himself are wide of the mark. The true understanding of sin is correlated with the knowledge of Jesus
Christ. ". . . only when we know Jesus Christ do we really
know that man is the man of sin, and what sin is, and what it
means for man."[114]

Barth depicts man's sin of pride by contrasting it with the
"obedience of the Son of God."[115] Man's pride manifests
itself in unbelief and disobedience. Whereas the incarnation

confronts us with God's condescension and self-humiliation, man in his pride seeks to exalt himself into the place of God. Or Barth can say that whereas the Lord became a servant, man in his sin is the servant who wants to be Lord. In contrast to Jesus Christ, the Judge who allowed himself to be judged for the sake of man, the proud sinner does not submit to God's judgment, desiring instead to be his own judge. In his death on the cross Jesus showed that trust in God which characterized him throughout his life; man in his pride, however, always thinks he can help and save himself.[116]

The proverb "Pride goes before a fall" is always true. "The fall of man comes in and with the pride of man. He falls in exalting himself where he ought not to try to exalt himself, where, according to the grace of God, he might in humility be freely and truly man." [117] While appreciative of certain emphases in the Augustinian doctrine of original sin, Barth holds that its development arose out of an improper combination of Psalm 51:7 and Romans 5:12. As a result, the concept of Adam's first sin was combined with the concept of inherited sin. Thus even though Barth affirms with Paul the solidarity of all men in sin, he finds no biblical support for teaching the biological transmission of Adam's sin and guilt to his posterity via procreation. Therefore, Barth like many other contemporary theologians interprets the story of Adam's fall as a saga which points to the experience of every man. "No one has to be Adam. We are so freely and on our own responsibility. Although the guilt of Adam is like ours, it is just as little our excuse as our guilt is his." [118] Nevertheless, with the Bible one can say that Adam is the exemplar and representative of all men. This means he did what all men do. The original sin of man is his first sin. For this and for his rebellion against God, each man is held accountable.[119]

In opposition to the views of Pelagius, Arminius, Socinius, the Enlightenment, and many Protestant liberals, Barth sides with the Reformers and the common testimony of the Scriptures in teaching that all men as sinners share a state of corruption. Hence the above traditions are wrong in speaking of capacities of man untouched by his sin or of some freedom of the will which he retains vis-à-vis God. Sin effects a total and radical perversion of human nature. The gravity of man's sin is established by the fact that God alone is able to forgive man. Man cannot do it. Forgiveness obtains only on the basis of the reconciling work of Jesus Christ which led to his death on the cross. When viewed in this light, it is impossible to exaggerate the extent and consequences of man's sin in terms of either his individual or his corporate existence. Each man is fallen, and humanity as a whole is enmeshed in a kingdom of evil.

In spite of his strong doctrine of man's fall and sin, Barth should not be accused of teaching that sin involves a total effacement of man's being in the image of God. Though some of Barth's early pronouncements might be interpreted in this way, he does not say this in the *Church Dogmatics*. Even as sinner, man remains God's creature. The following statement is typical: "However we may describe the fallen being of man, we cannot say that man is fallen completely away from God, in the sense that he is lost to Him or that he has perished." [120] Uninformed critics of Barth should read him carefully at this point! His obvious concern is to avoid a dualism in which man's sin and the power of evil become insuperable obstacles to the movement of God's grace in Jesus Christ. That is to say, man's corruption cannot be greater than, different from, or less than that which was overcome in Christ's atoning work on the cross. [121] Barth therefore always magnifies the "triumph of grace" over man's sin. He can say:

> Still much more true than our "unfreedom," still more true than the sad truth of our *servum arbitrium* [enslaved will], is the joyous truth that God is free to be, and to remain, and to be ever anew the One who has created man, the gracious God, the One who is free to allow man to be that which He has created him to be, namely, the creature to whom He is merciful. [122]

THE JUSTIFICATION OF MAN

It is important to note where Barth treats the doctrine of justification.[123] In contrast to Lutheranism which makes this doctrine central for the entire content and structure of theology, Barth seems to reflect the emphasis of the Reformed tradition in stressing the sovereignty of God and man's justification resulting from it. Barth's understanding is that God's eternal gracious decree to save man through Jesus Christ is the ultimate ground of man's justification. The manner in which God's saving purpose for humanity is effected through Jesus Christ is the subject of the entire doctrine of reconciliation. Man's justification is wholly dependent upon what God does in the life, death, and resurrection of the God-man, Jesus Christ. His saving purpose has been accomplished because the Lord became a servant and this servant was exalted as Lord. What Jesus did, therefore, manifests a divine judgment and verdict which effects man's justification. Therefore, in order to speak correctly about man's justification, Barth points first—in his customary fashion—to what God does *objectively* to bring this about in Jesus Christ; then he proceeds to show how through faith man acknowledges *subjectively* what God in Christ has done for the world and for him, too. This procedure is evident in the thesis with which Barth summarizes the justification of man.

> The right of God established in the death of Jesus Christ, and proclaimed in His resurrection in defiance of the wrong of man, is as such the basis of the new and corresponding right of man. Promised to man in Jesus Christ, hidden in Him and only to be revealed in Him, it cannot be attained by any thought or effort or achievement on the part of man. But the reality of it calls for faith in every man as a suitable acknowledgment and appropriation and application.[124]

A few statements are in order concerning the way in which the sinner is justified. Man is radically fallen and unable to contribute to his salvation. If he is made right with God, it must be because of something God has done. How does this occur?

(1) First, man's transition from death to life takes place because God is true to his eternal purpose by realizing his loving and gracious will in Jesus Christ. God, the Creator and covenant-partner of man, does not relinquish his claim upon sinful humanity. Man's sin and injustice are not greater than God's justice and grace. Therefore, God intervenes to overcome man's injustice and the power of sin by acting in keeping with his own being as Creator and Lord. By effecting man's justification, he does that which is right and just; i.e., he acts in accord with his own being and will. Barth paraphrases Romans 3:26 as follows: "In this work of the justification of unrighteous man God also and in the first instance justifies Himself." [125]

(2) The divine judgment by which man is justified is not simply a divine declaration. It is that, but it is more. It is God's gracious judgment which is enacted in Jesus Christ. God humbles himself in his Son to the point of death upon the cross, thereby taking upon himself the judgment which sinful man deserves. Jesus is fully obedient to his Father's will and to his mission; he bears the sins of all men in enduring suffering, rejection, and death on their behalf. In this way man's sin against God is done away with. Jesus Christ, the righteous one, suffered on behalf of all the unrighteous. This is the divine judgment which brings about the liberation and acquittal of the sinner. This is the manifestation of the righteousness of God which effects the forgiveness of our sin against God.

(3) In order for man's transition from the life of the old man to that of the new to be complete, there must be a new or righteous or justified man. This man is Jesus Christ raised from the dead. Thus even as the death of the old man has to be referred to Jesus Christ who acts as our representative, so the life of the new man is seen in him whose resurrection is

the sign of the vindication of God's purpose and the beginning of a new humanity. This is the positive side of our justification; by raising Jesus Christ from the dead, God affirmed
what Jesus Christ had done in his death. Thus the purpose of
God which is hidden in the death of Jesus is revealed in his
resurrection. Moreover, since Jesus Christ is also our representative in his resurrection, his vindication is ours as well.
Therefore, our transition from death to life—our justification—is actual only in and through Jesus Christ. Barth holds
that this transition is never assured if we look at ourselves;
it is grounded neither in our experience nor in what we do.
"Our justification is all true and actual in Him and therefore
in us. It cannot, therefore, be known to be valid and effective
in us first, but in Him first, and because in Him in us." [126]
Because it is effective in Jesus Christ, "we have a future and
hope, the door has been opened, and we cross the threshold
from wrong to right, and therefore from death to life." [127]

(4) We have seen that Jesus Christ is the source of man's
justification. Man is justified by clinging in faith to Jesus
Christ and his righteousness. Barth affirms with the Reformers that we are justified by the "strange" or "alien" righteousness of Jesus Christ. Faith which is directed toward any
other being or power cannot justify. Barth also agrees with
Luther's emphasis that within man's temporal life, he will
always view himself as sinner and justified at the same time.
However, man is to listen to the divine promise of the reality
of (a) the forgiveness of his sins in the present and in the
future. The content of God's promise to man and therefore
the completion of his justification also means (b) that man
enters into a relationship with God which is not only that oʾ
the creature, but also that of a child of God. Finally, to rely
on the promise of God means (c) that the justified man may
live in hope. He is "born anew to a living hope through the
resurrection of Jesus Christ from the dead" (1 Pet. 1:3, RSV).
The Christian pilgrim looks to the fulfillment of God's promise when he will be no longer simultaneously sinner and jus-

tified. In that day, he will be wholly justified. "To have the forgiveness of sins and to be a child of God means to be one who awaits this inheritance and moves towards it."[128]

Jesus Christ, the Servant as Lord

THE EXALTATION OF THE SON OF MAN

We move to the second christological thesis at the heart of the doctrine of reconciliation, which Barth entitles "Jesus Christ, the Servant as Lord." It is not enough to speak of the Lord who became a servant in the incarnation, humbling himself even to death on the cross for the salvation of mankind. To be sure, we had to speak first of God's movement toward us in his Son; there we were concerned with the movement from "above to below." But God's reconciling work also includes the exaltation of Jesus Christ, the servant and Son of Man, to be the Lord. Here the movement is from "below to above." Moreover, even as Jesus Christ is the representative of all men in his humiliation, suffering, and death, so, too, his exaltation as the Son of Man involves the exaltation of humanity. Thus, the human nature which he assumed in the incarnation in order to redeem it—in accordance with God's eternal purpose—moves homeward to God in his public exaltation as the Son of Man attested in his resurrection and ascension.

Barth develops the kingly work of Jesus Christ by speaking of the "Homecoming of the Son of Man." Our reconciliation is completed by virtue of our inclusion in the humanity of the Son of Man, the servant who is declared the Lord. "The humiliation of God and the exaltation of man as they took place in Him [Jesus Christ] are the completed fulfillment of the covenant, the completed reconciliation of the world with God."[129]

The basis for our exaltation also can be seen in the fact that Jesus Christ is the "Royal Man." He is the Second Adam. His existence in the world reflects the attitude of God toward man. Barth writes:

The man Jesus is the royal man in the fact that He is not
merely one man with others but *the* man for them (as God
is for them), the man in whom the love and faithfulness and
salvation and glory of God are addressed to man in the concrete form of a historical relationship of man to man: and
this in spite of their own adamic form. . . . The man Jesus
is decisively created after God in the fact that He is as man
the work and revelation of the mercy of God, of His Gospel,
His kingdom of peace, His atonement, and that He is His
creaturely and earthly and historical correspondence in this
sense.[130]

Barth concludes his treatment of the kingly work of Jesus
Christ, the Son of God who became the Son of Man, by speaking of the "Direction of the Son." Because the eternal Son
became true man in the incarnation and as the Son of Man is
the brother of all men, and because the Son of Man is the
Lord, a power flows from his existence which gives humanity
a new direction. What he effected as the Son of Man in his
life, death, resurrection, and exaltation to the Father gives
humanity a new direction. The victory of his humiliation and
exaltation is efficacious in effecting both our justification or
forgiveness and our sanctification. The continuing power
which derives from his saving work is made effectual through
the presence of the Holy Spirit who reveals to us our new
being in Jesus Christ. The Holy Spirit is also responsible for
instructing us concerning the new direction which we have
been given and to which we have been exalted in Jesus Christ,
the Son of Man.

Barth summarizes what is involved in speaking of "Jesus
Christ, the Servant as Lord," or the "Exaltation of the Son of
Man," thus:

Jesus Christ, the Son of God and Lord who humbled Himself
to be a servant, is also the Son of Man exalted as this servant
to be the Lord, the new and true and royal man who participates in the being and life and lordship and act of God and
honours and attests Him, and as such the Head and Repre-

sentative and Saviour of all other men, the origin and content and norm of the divine direction given us in the work of the Holy Spirit.[131]

THE SANCTIFICATION OF MAN

The event of reconciliation in Jesus Christ is the basis both of man's justification and his sanctification. We have seen that man's justification is inextricably tied to the humiliation of God in his Son in which he affirms "I will be your God." When man acknowledges in faith his justification, this is the first moment of reconciliation. But we have seen that reconciliation also includes the exaltation of the Son of Man and by it man's exaltation. This is man's sanctification through Jesus Christ, and the second moment of God's reconciling work. Here God speaks the words, "Ye shall be my people." Barth's concern in the doctrine of sanctification is to show how God through Jesus Christ has turned man toward himself and given him a new direction in life, namely, Godward. Man's response through obedience and love represents the attempt to reflect and correspond to "the holiness imparted to him in Jesus Christ."[132]

There are several dangers concerning the relationship of justification and sanctification Barth wants to avoid. First, man's sanctification cannot mean that by doing good works man eventually merits justification. God is the one who sanctifies man through Jesus Christ. The holiness of the Christian can never be understood apart from God's act in Jesus Christ. This false approach may lead to a kind of activism which does not recognize that the beginning and continuance of man's sanctification are due to the work of God in Jesus Christ and through his Spirit. Secondly, one can stress God's grace to such an extent that man's response is completely neglected and negated. Here sanctification is swallowed up in justification. In this view, God alone is at work in isolation from man. This leads to Quietism.

It is Barth's contention that neither justification nor sanctification has a temporal priority over the other, since both take place through the one act of God in the humiliation and exaltation of Jesus Christ. However, if we ask about the structure or substance of God's reconciling action, it can be said that justification has the priority. That is, it is on the basis of being forgiven through Jesus Christ and accepting God's gracious judgment declared in him (justification) that man has the possibility of living as his disciple (sanctification). On the other hand, Barth contends that since God's will for man is a life of obedient service, his sanctification, the latter precedes justification in terms of God's will, purpose, and goal for man.

From this perspective, Barth unfolds the content of man's sanctification. The briefest mention of the characteristics of the life of the Christian must suffice here.

(1) Saints are those who share in the holiness of Jesus Christ, the "Holy One." Through being related to him, Christians are aware that they are still not yet fully redeemed. More important, however, is the truth that even as sinners they are enabled through the power of his Spirit to serve him obediently in the world.

(2) Sanctification therefore involves the "Call to Discipleship." This means to live in response to Jesus' call and summons—not to some program, system, or idea about God or Jesus Christ. This discipleship involves personal decision and self-denial as one lives as a witness of God's love for the whole world.

(3) In order for discipleship to be a reality, there must be an "Awakening to Conversion." This awakening from the "sleep of death" is effected through God's sanctifying power while at the same time calling forth man's total response. Conversion does not refer to one event at the beginning of the Christian's life, but has to do with the new direction of his life as he lives in obedience toward Jesus Christ and thus in the service of God.

(4) To live the life of the sanctified involves doing good

works. In this way, Christians offer their praise unto God—
and their works reflect God's good works in creation and
reconciliation.

(5) Finally, the life of discipleship means Christians live
"with the mark of the cross . . . laid upon them." In no way
does the Christian's identification with the sufferings and
death of Jesus Christ replace the latter's significance. Yet the
sign of the cross which Christians bear is part and parcel of
their existence in this life; ultimately, however, man's hopes
will be realized in the resurrection of the dead and the life
of fuller fellowship with the Lord.[133]

Throughout the doctrine of reconciliation Barth affirms
that God as Holy Spirit manifests himself first of all to his
community, the church, and then to individuals only as they
are members of the Body of Christ. This precludes speaking
of man's justification, sanctification, or calling apart from
his inclusion in the Christian community. In this way Barth
avoids the illegitimate individualism and subjectivism which
has frequently characterized Protestantism.

Jesus Christ, the True Witness

We come to the final christological thesis of Barth's doctrine of reconciliation, which he titles "Jesus Christ, the True
Witness." We have seen that God's reconciling activity must
be understood in terms of (1) the humiliation of the Lord
who became a servant and (2) the exaltation of this servant
or the Son of Man as the Lord. In one sense, the act of God in
Jesus Christ to which we pointed in these two propositions
says everything necessary about man's salvation accomplished
through Jesus Christ. Thus, in turning to Christ's prophetic
work nothing is added to his reconciling work. Rather, Barth's
concern is to show how what Jesus Christ has done for man's
salvation is communicated to man through his prophetic work
and the activity of the Holy Spirit which attests him.

The "Glory of the Mediator" is seen in that Jesus is "The
Light of Life." This is because he is God present with us,
because he is the eternal Word of God which became flesh.

His life, death, and resurrection attest that he is indeed the "Light of the World" before whom all other lights appear dim. This same Jesus Christ is the risen Lord of the world he has reconciled. He makes himself known through the words of his witnesses in the Scriptures and in the preaching and teaching of the church. But even beyond the normal media which reflect and attest Jesus Christ as the "Light of Life," there are lesser lights in creation—events in history, nature, and human existence—which in their way may point to him. This is due to the fact that the creation is ordained to be the theater in which the glory of God is revealed. In no way, however, should these lesser lights in the created order be interpreted so as to detract from the significance of Jesus Christ. Therefore, in interpreting God's reconciling love, Barth reaffirms the stance of Barmen and his own christo-centrism in maintaining that, "Jesus Christ . . . is the one Word of God. . . ."[134]

Barth borrows the phrase of the elder Blumhardt, "Jesus is Victor," as an apt description of the way Jesus Christ pursues his prophetic ministry. By virtue of the reconciliation he accomplished, Jesus is already victor! However, he continues the prophetic work begun during his earthly ministry by calling man through his Word to acknowledge the reconciliation which has been effected for all men. He calls them from darkness into his light. He confronts the powers which oppose him and hold men captive, and he continues to triumph over them. The fact that powers of evil still oppose him and that many men do not acknowledge their salvation through him should not be cause for despair. Jesus Christ is victor! The final and ultimate victory is not yet; but because of who he is and what he has done, that victory is assured.[135]

In the interim between his resurrection and final coming, Christ makes himself known in the world through his Spirit. His resurrection marks the beginning of his permeation of the world with his glory in a way not possible during his earthly ministry. Until the time of his return, Christ through his Spirit is effectively present and active, liberating men so that they may acknowledge him as their reconciler. Thereby believers are enabled to live in hope and to hope for others who do not yet believe. They can do this with joy because God has reconciled the world to himself through Christ and he will win the ultimate victory in his final coming.[136]

Jesus Christ is active as man's contemporary through his Word and his Spirit, awakening and calling men to a life of discipleship. Once again, the initiative lies with God. He is responsible both for the initial calling of Christians and for sustaining and directing them as his sons. They are followers of Jesus Christ who trust and acknowledge him and live under his Lordship by obeying his Word. The fellowship which Christ establishes between himself and his followers does not obliterate the distinction between him as Lord and believers as his servants and disciples. Nor will Barth allow the Christian's calling to be restricted to the advancement of his personal piety. Though the transformation of the believer's personal existence is important, it is more important to recognize that he is called to participate in God's mission of reconciliation in the world. This is what Barth means in saying that Christ calls the Christian "thrusting him as His afflicted but well-equipped witness into the service of his prophetic work."[137]

The most comprehensive description of the Christian is that of a witness. His calling is to attest through word and deed the reconciling love of God in Jesus Christ for the whole world. He is able to make this witness because he has been set free to do so through the power of God. This may and often will entail suffering affliction at the hands of the world. Nevertheless, this fact should not lead to despair. The Christian's concern should be to be obedient to his commission and mission, recognizing that God is always faithful. What God has done in Jesus Christ, what he now does through his Spirit, and what he has promised to do in the future is adequate to effect the reconciliation, calling, and equipping of all of his disciples, and indeed, of the whole world.[138]

In bringing his treatment of the doctrine of reconciliation

to a close, Barth deals with "The Holy Spirit and the Sending of the Christian Community." Since it recapitulates some of the emphases already noted, it may be cited without comment.

> The Holy Spirit is the enlightening power of the living Lord Jesus Christ in which He confesses the community called by Him as His body, i.e., as His own earthly-historical form of existence, by entrusting to it the ministry of His prophetic Word and therefore the provisional representation of the calling of all humanity and indeed of all creatures as it has taken place in Him. He does this by sending it among the peoples as His own people, ordained for its part to confess Him before all men, to call them to Him and thus to make known to the whole world that the covenant between God and man concluded in Him is the first and final meaning of its history, and that His future manifestation is already here and now its great, effective and living hope.[139]

IV. Interpreting
Barth's Significance

It cannot be the purpose of this brief epilogue to analyze the numerous and often conflicting assessments which continue to be made of the theology of Karl Barth. During the past fifty years in which his theology has exercised a significant influence upon the course of modern theology, his position has attracted many and repelled others. A mark of his greatness in contemporary theology is evidenced by the fact that the history of theology in this century to date is unintelligible apart from him. Moreover, his sharpest critics acknowledge his contribution, and even today no theologian can afford to by-pass his thought. This must be said even though there are signs—to borrow the phrase which H. R. Mackintosh applied to Albrecht Ritschl—that Barth's theology is behind a "passing cloud."

Whether future generations will regard Barth's theological perspective and position as the most significant in the twentieth century must remain an open question. It is more relevant to note that Barth's approach has been so pervasive because his own theological pilgrimage involved his confrontation with and critique of Protestant liberalism which had dominated Protestant theology for over a century. One of the decisive issues which Barth's theology raises is whether his interpretation of nineteenth-century liberalism is adequate and fair.

A further factor accounting for Barth's dominant influence

upon the direction of theology in this century derives from the breadth of his theological interests and competence. The indices of the *Church Dogmatics* reveal his continuing dialogue with both the witness of Holy Scripture and the major movements in the history of theology and philosophy to the present. His lifelong interest in Roman Catholic theology continues to attract attention among Roman Catholics. In his careful study of Barth's theology, Balthasar contends that Barth must be chosen as the Protestant partner in the Roman Catholic-Protestant dialogue "because in his work authentic Protestantism has found its full-blown image *for the first time*."[1] He goes on to say that Roman Catholicism finds in "Barth's *Dogmatics* . . . a theology that is coextensive with ours in history and subject matter."[2] Barth kept abreast of developments in Roman Catholicism until his death, and one of his last writings was *Ad Limina Apostolorum: An Appraisal of Vatican II.*

In spite of numerous studies of Barth's theology, of which this introduction is yet another, the reader seeking a reliable perspective from which to interpret Barth's system as a whole is faced with numerous difficulties.

(1) First, he is confronted with countless suggestions concerning the key which will unlock the intricacies of Barth's thought. Among those encountered most frequently are: dialectical theology, theology of crisis, theology of the Word of God, neoorthodoxy, neoreformation theology, biblicism, and christomonism. The problem at this point is compounded because of the sheer massiveness of the *Church Dogmatics.* Whoever suggests such a key must have an intimate knowledge of the total system. In contending that Barth's theology is best understood in terms of his pervasive christocentrism, we find support both among his Protestant and Catholic interpreters. To designate the bent of his theology in this way, however, neither enables the reader to anticipate Barth's conclusions nor spares him the necessity of coming to grips with Barth's thought for himself.

(2) Second, in attempting to understand Barth, the reader

should deal critically with analyses written before or at the very beginning of the *Church Dogmatics*. In the course of our study we have alluded to certain standard misconceptions of Barth's thought still being offered by interpreters who have read very little of his mature writings, or who base their conclusions on Barth's *Epistle to the Romans* published in 1922! In our approach the attempt has been made to show something of the development of Barth's theology from its beginnings to its most recent expression in the *Church Dogmatics*.

(3) A third problem confronting the interpreter of Barth is whether the key to his thought lies in his earlier or later writings. Some critics speak about the "late" or "new" Barth, distinguishing the mature Barth of the *Church Dogmatics* from the "early" Barth of the *Romans*. Some of these critics see discontinuity rather than continuity between the early and late Barth. We find ourselves more in agreement with those who see a basic continuity in his theological development. This does not deny what Barth has referred to as the increasing "christological concentration" in his thought, or even some quite obvious corrections which Barth himself made looking back on his earlier formulations. We maintain, therefore, that there is a basic continuity in Barth's theological perspective and approach from the time of the *Romans* to his mature dogmatics. In its most general form, the thread running throughout Barth's writings is the emphasis upon the priority and sovereignty of God and his critique of all theologies which in any way detract from that sovereignty.

With these points in mind, the student investigating Barth's theology will avoid utilizing superficial labels to characterize it. He should reserve hasty judgment concerning Barth's theological program, recognizing among other things that his theology should not be identified with that of avowed "Barthians" whose approach is usually far less creative than their mentor's. He must remember that Barth is heavily indebted to the witness of the Bible, and especially to the Apostle Paul, but that he is not the advocate of a wooden biblicism. He will recall Barth's appreciation of the theology of the Reformers and even of Protestant Orthodoxy at certain points, while not equating his theology with a simple restatement of either. Barth's lifelong critique of Protestant liberalism will always be in evidence, but this should not blind the interpreter to Barth's recognition of some of its contributions. Indeed, one may well ask whether Barth himself ever fully acknowledged his debt to the liberal theology in which he was nurtured.

BARTH'S POSITIVE CONTRIBUTIONS

(1) Whatever attitude one takes toward the theology of Karl Barth, it cannot be forgotten that he precipitated a revolution in modern theology. Though other important theologians joined him in establishing this new theological front, Barth led the way. A sign of his stature is evidenced by the fact that virtually every theological position he developed has influenced the course of contemporary theology. This holds true for his mode of biblical interpretation, his doctrine of revelation and his rejection of natural theology, his view of God and his relationship to man and the world, the manner in which he conceives of the task of theology and its relationship to philosophy, his doctrine of election, as well as his christology, anthropology, and ethics.

(2) In our study we have seen how Barth tried to stem the tide of modern Protestant theology which was in danger of concentrating more upon man than upon God and God's revelation of himself. We have referred to this tradition as anthropological theology—that mode of theologizing in which man is the "centre and measure and goal of all things." [3] Throughout his long career, Barth taught that the church and Christian theology must begin and end with its attention fixed upon the Word of God, that is, upon what God has done in the past, is doing in the present, and will yet do in the future to complete his saving purpose in the world. In attempting to be obedient to what Holy Scripture says concerning God's revelation of himself, Barth developed a theological vision which is strongly theocentric and christocentric. He de-

scribed the difference between this approach and that of
Protestant liberalism as follows: ". . . we have met God, we
have heard His Word—that is the original and ultimate fact.
The movement of thought here is not from below upwards
but from above downwards."[4] Whether one agrees with
Barth's theocentric or christocentric theology and methodology or not, one cannot deny the creative and consistent expression which he has given this position in the face of all
detractors.

(3) Barth's new perspective was inextricably bound up
with the creative way in which he reasserted the authority of
Holy Scripture for the church within the context of his doctrine of the Word of God. In so doing he reasserted the position
of the Protestant Reformers. Moreover, he did so in the face of
the gradual erosion of the Bible's authority in modern Protestantism from about 1800 on. In view of questions raised
about the authority of the Bible from the rise of biblical
criticism, modern Protestant theologians attempted to ground
theology upon some more certain and defensible foundation.
Generally speaking they moved in the direction of subjectivism. Hence, the task of theology became that of interpreting
the Christian's religious consciousness, piety, religious experience, or perhaps his moral consciousness. By proceeding in
this manner, the theologian sought to by-pass the primacy of
the authority of the Scriptures for the church's teaching and
preaching as it had been customarily affirmed in Protestantism. In Barth's estimate, the demise of the Bible's authority
in modern Protestantism went hand in hand with scepticism
and uncertainty concerning the reality of revelation or the
possibility of any true knowledge of God. Again, whether one
agrees with Barth or not, it cannot be denied that his theological position encouraged the reassertion of the centrality
of Holy Scripture as the primary norm which guides, nur-
tures, and reforms the church's faith and life. Moreover, he
based his theology upon the priority of the Bible's authority
as the primary written witness to God's revelation of himself

in an age when religious relativism and pluralism were generally presupposed.

In this connection it must not be forgotten that Barth's theology is inextricably bound up with a particular mode of biblical interpretation. From the first edition of his *Römerbrief* (1919) to the final page of the *Church Dogmatics,* Barth's hermeneutics is apparent. For Barth, the concerns paramount in the historical-critical study of the Scriptures are significant. Everything possible must be done through the use of lower and higher criticism to recover the text, the *Sitz im Leben* (context) of the biblical writings, and the manner of their transmission. One should not stop there, however. Nor should one move in the direction of Bultmann's existentialistic mode of interpretation by assuming that the biblical writers' primary concern is to relate their own self-understanding. Rather, the exegete must seek to uncover the "text within the text" or the "Word within the words." That is, biblical exegesis must concern itself first and last with the manner and the extent to which the biblical witnesses point to revelation, to the Word of God. For Barth, this was their primary and overriding intention. Barth's exegesis is directed to this end and his method of biblical exposition continues to play an important role in contemporary biblical interpretation.[5]

(4) It is to Barth's credit that his *Church Dogmatics* helped to reestablish the significance of theology in the life of the church. At the beginning of this century, systematic theology was in a sad state of decline, especially in the United States. Philosophy of religion, comparative religion, and related disciplines had either replaced dogmatics in the curriculum of theological seminaries or forced it into a position of subsidiary importance. Barth's insistence that theology should be the servant, facilitating the witness, teaching and preaching of the church, encouraged many pastors and theologians in their respective ministries. In addition, Barth pursued the theological task with such creativity and energy

that he helped make it possible for theology to resume its legitimate place within the academic community as a scientific discipline.

(5) In addition to the renaissance of exegesis and biblical theology which Barth's theology helped precipitate, one must recall that from first to last he intended his theology to undergird the preaching of the church. No contemporary theologian has related dogmatics and preaching as intimately as he. This is due in part to the fact that Barth was led to a new theological position as he reflected upon, and engaged in, the exegesis and exposition of the Scriptures while a pastor involved in preaching. This interest is also evident in the *Church Dogmatics*—a veritable treasure of biblical exegesis and exposition, as every careful reader will know. Barth's concern for the content of the church's proclamation gives his theology a decidedly pastoral tone at many points. Hence, Barth's struggle to recover the meaning of the Bible's witness to revelation was not an academic exercise removed from any relationship to the life of the church; it was undertaken to strengthen and to refine the church's witness through preaching. Shortly before his death, Barth spoke concerning this matter on a radio broadcast: "Really, my entire theology is essentially a theology for preachers. It arose out of my own situation (as a pastor) in which I was called upon to instruct, preach and engage a bit in the pastoral care of souls."[6]

(6) The contributions described thus far have to do primarily with Barth's perspective and method of doing theology. In turning to the doctrinal areas in which his theology has been influential, one must single out first his doctrine of God. In his refusal to equate the God attested in the Bible with God or gods known through other revelations and means, Barth took a significant step. It involved a sharp break with a prevalent tradition in both Roman Catholic and Protestant theology which allows for the equation of the concept of ultimate Being or God arrived at via reason, philosophical speculation, intuition, or man's religious quest with the living God of the Bible. The biblical God is not a static

and timeless being; he is the triune God who reveals himself actively as Father, Son, and Holy Spirit. Contemporary Catholic and Protestant attempts to interpret the nature of God so as to avoid the liabilities attaching to static hellenistic conceptions of his nature so typical of traditional formulations are all indebted to Barth's dynamic conception of God. In opposition to some contemporaries, Barth constructed his doctrine of God in the light of God's acts rather than by beginning with a discussion of God's being as he is in himself. However, Barth will not allow the stress upon God's immanence in his revelation to be interpreted in such a way that he ceases to be who he is. That is, God is never to be identified with the world or with man, even though he is present in his Son who is man for the benefit of the whole world. God remains the sovereign and transcendent Lord who loves in freedom; he is the eternal God who is Lord of past, present, and future, and therefore the only ground of man's hope.[7]

(7) Although we have already alluded to Barth's concentration upon the revelation of God in Jesus Christ as determinative of his total theological orientation, we must single out this dominant characteristic for special mention as perhaps his most significant contribution. The objectivity and concreteness of Barth's theology stems from his continual engagement with the interpretation of the revelation of God in Jesus Christ. No theologian in the history of the church has interpreted the nature of God and all of his relationships to man and the universe in terms of his self-revelation in Jesus Christ as rigorously as has Barth. He classifies all talk of God which by-passes God who is "for us" and "with us" in his Son and in his Spirit as abstract. Accordingly, he rejects attempts to arrive at knowledge of God by means of natural theology or by beginning with the perception of God on the basis of his revelation of himself in creation or in man. God graciously condescends to man in his Son and through his Spirit: this is the sole basis for all past, present, and future knowledge of him.

(8) One of Barth's distinctive contributions is related to

the foregoing. We saw earlier that because of the way he sees God's eternal electing love actualized in the incarnation of the Son, his theology takes on a comprehensiveness which is hardly surpassed in Christian history. Creation, providence and preservation, the covenant history fulfilled in Jesus Christ, the Son's reconciling work, the existence of the church and of Christians, and the movement of all things towards their consummation through Jesus Christ in the future—all of this hangs together and is determined by the divine predestination.

(9) Though we have not been able to pursue Barth's contributions in the area of ethics, it is well known that he has done much to avoid an unhealthy bifurcation between dogmatics and ethics in contemporary theology by dealing with general and special ethics throughout the *Church Dogmatics*. Thomas C. Oden notes that Barth's ethic is currently attracting more attention than his doctrinal statements and predicts that it will become increasingly relevant. In part, this is due to the fact that Barth grappled with the meaning of God's command and the revelation of God in Jesus Christ as the basis for understanding man's responsibility and action in the world. Oden is right in characterizing the heart of Barth's ethic as follows: "The freedom of God for man, and the corresponding freedom of man for God and for all others, is the core theme of Barth's ethic."[8] God's action in man's behalf in Jesus Christ has liberated man from enslavement to self and lesser lords in order that he may make use of the new freedom granted him to live as God's covenant-partner. The Christian fulfills God's will in the world as he responds in freedom to God's gracious commandment by honoring God and by utilizing his freedom as God's child to live for his neighbor.

(10) Some mention should be made of Barth's Christian humanism in this list of positive contributions. Today men are grappling with the meaning of individual and corporate existence. Increasingly, a secular humanism which interprets man without reference to God claims to provide the most

adequate interpretation of human existence. It is to Barth's credit that he developed such a powerful Christian humanism. In doing so, he corrected a certain pessimism characteristic of some of his earlier statements. In view of the "humanity" of God manifest in Jesus Christ, we saw that Barth has a very positive view of human nature. All men are to be understood in the light of God's love for mankind in Jesus Christ. What is more, since culture is the expression of man's collective humanity, one should not negate its positive values and achievements made possible through God's sustenance and grace. This is the basis of Barth's great appreciation for the music of Mozart. Thus, it is quite wrong to charge Barth with being a pessimist with respect to man and culture. Quite the contrary is true: since Barth sees man and culture in the light of Jesus Christ, one can say that he is among the most "secular" theologians of our day. Though not usually acknowledged, it is probably true that the affirmation of the secular and the secular relevance of the gospel by the radical theologians owes some debt to Karl Barth. But unlike the latter and all others who want to speak of man and culture without reference to God, Barth writes:

> Since God in His deity is human, this culture [i.e., *theological* culture] must occupy itself neither with God in Himself nor with man in himself, but with man-encountering God and the God-encountering man and with their dialogue and history, in which their communion takes place and comes to its fulfillment.[9]

(11) In the midst of the current revival of eschatology and the rise of the theology of hope, it must be recalled that the early Barth and his colleagues were the first theologians in this century to recognize the theological significance of the recovery of the eschatological perspective of the New Testament by Albert Schweitzer and Johannes Weiss around 1900. It may well be true that Barth's understanding of biblical eschatology in its cosmic dimensions was more adequate in

the first edition of his commentary on Romans than in the
second. Yet in the latter, he made this programmatic statement: "If Christianity be not altogether thoroughgoing eschatology, there remains in it no relationship whatever with
Christ." [10]

SOME CRITICAL QUESTIONS

(1) One of the major points at which Barth has come under
attack relates to his refusal to admit that God's universal
revelation of himself to all men in creation in human nature itself may issue in some true knowledge of God. Ever
since his debate with Emil Brunner in 1934 over general
revelation and natural theology, Barth has been interpreted
as an implacable foe of both. His refusal to allow for the
possibility of saving knowledge of God in non-Christian religions is related to and consistent with this position.

With respect to all of this, the critics ask: does not Barth's
position conflict with the scriptural teaching affirming God's
universal revelation? They also find Barth's interpretation
of the intention of those affirming a natural theology rather
strained. That is, many advocates of natural theology would
not speak of man's "unaided" ascent to God via God's preliminary manifestations of himself. Instead, they maintain
that whenever man knows God—whether through the historical Mediator or through God's approach to man in creation—
we are dealing with God's initiative and grace. Furthermore,
if creation is already prepared for God's grace and if Christ
as the eternal logos is active in creation as the later Barth
insists, then must not the possibility be left open that there
may be some positive response by man to God's approach in
creation? Does not Barth point in this direction in teaching
that man always remains related to God even as sinner? Even
if it is true that Barth's emphasis upon man's sinful propen-
sities negates the saving value of the light of God which shines
everywhere in his creation, it appears that Barth's position
is more restrictive than that of the Scriptures.

(2) A more fundamental criticism has to do with the pervasive christocentrism in Barth's theology. Here we can do no more than pose the question. One way to ask it is as follows: does Barth's theology derive from a legitimate interpretation of the revelation of God attested in Holy Scripture or are certain philosophical presuppositions actually determinative? We must remember that Barth criticizes Bultmann and others for allowing philosophical presuppositions to distort the way in which God's revelation is interpreted. With Balthasar and others we must ask: has not Barth allowed certain categories and tendencies of German philosophical idealism to influence the manner in which he interprets the Scriptures? Is his christocentric doctrine of election a legitimate interpretation of Scripture or is it an indication that Barth succumbed to metaphysical speculation and to the concern for the all-encompassing system so dear to the idealists such as Hegel and Schleiermacher? Is not Barth truly the great systematician in the line of German philosophical idealism? There are indications that some of the categories Barth borrows from philosophical idealism have been "baptized" for theological usage, but the question remains whether they are appropriate to express the biblical witness to revelation.

The fact that numerous critics have charged Barth with christomonism or an illegitimate christocentrism raises a cluster of issues. The basic question is whether Barth's depiction of creation, history, human existence, and all things pertaining to the relationship between God and man can be derived so strictly and logically from the conception of God's eternal election and predestination. Is not Barth guilty of metaphysical speculation in basing the whole story of man's relationship to God from creation to the *eschaton* on a few scriptural statements which relate Christ to God's saving intention even prior to the creation of the world? It seems at times that Barth calls in question even the relative independence of creation, human history, and human freedom—which he elsewhere affirms—in his desire to show that what occurs in human history and in the history of Jesus Christ has been determined in advance in the counsel of God. Is Barth not guilty of allowing the person of Jesus Christ—the electing God—to operate as a systematic principle in order that the entire system might be completely consistent and harmonious? Barth's tendencies in this direction account for the further contention that he is guilty of excessive systematization. This gives one the impression that Barth's theology has fallen down from heaven. Balthasar puts this point nicely in saying that at times it seems that Barth has looked into "God's cards." He seems to know at the beginning or the end of theological reflection what seems knowable only when faith becomes sight. If this is the case, theology is in control of revelation rather than in process of following after its object.[11]

(3) An issue related to the foregoing has to do with Barth's universalistic tendencies. Has Barth been forced in this direction because of the way in which he has understood the eternal divine election? To be sure, Barth refuses to teach universal salvation directly. Nevertheless, it is the logically necessary outcome of his doctrine of election and his view of reconciliation based thereon. Here again we are faced with a position which tends to relativize man's sin and the possibility of final judgment and separation from God. It would seem that Barth is in danger of restricting the freedom of God as well as the limited freedom of man.

In this connection, something of a puzzle remains with respect to the objective reconciliation effected by God for all men in Jesus Christ and the subjective appropriation thereof by man. On the one hand, Barth speaks as though everything necessary for man's reconciliation with God has been accomplished by Jesus Christ. On the other hand, he depicts the work of the Holy Spirit as the completion or fulfillment of God's reconciling work. Is it possible to speak of reconciliation being accomplished through Jesus Christ without talking of man's appropriation? Does Barth hold these two emphases in balance? Moreover, since some do not as yet believe, is this due to a restriction in God's love—which Barth denies— or is it due to man's recalcitrance and his refusal of God's love which can lead to final judgment—which Barth also appears to rule out? These are issues in which certain ambiguities remain in Barth's thought.

(4) Although we have seen that Barth attempted to contrast the biblical view of the living God with a static conception of God characteristic of the Greek tradition, Moltmann and others find Barth still too addicted to Greek categories. Therefore, they see a tendency in Barth to interpret God's revelation of himself too much in terms of the idea of the eternal present in time, and of the correspondence between man and God which this makes possible, instead of understanding revelation "from the standpoint of the promise contained in the revelation." [12] We may express this more generally in saying that Barth is criticized for failing to do justice to the eschatological perspective of the Christian faith. This is perhaps but another way of saying that Barth's doctrine of the triune God and his eternal predestination does not do justice to the unfinished nature of God's revelation and the corresponding futuristic perspective of the New Testament. Moltmann is right in his contention that in the thought of Barth the future consummation for which the church hopes seems often to be nothing more than the further unveiling of the eternal divine purpose or of the significance of the revelation of God which has already occurred in Jesus Christ. Barth's mode of thinking is retrospective rather than prospective. In this way there is a failure to appreciate fully the movement of God in history, the openness of human existence and history, and the nature of the church as the exodus community which lives and works as God's pilgrim people in the hope of the coming kingdom of God. In bringing these themes to powerful expression in contemporary theology, the theology of hope does greater justice to the futuristic and forward-looking thrust of the Christian faith which comes into existence because of the resurrection of Jesus Christ from the dead. In developing more fully the meaning of the Christian hope and the significance of the kingdom of God for understanding the present and future hope of the church, man, and

human history, the theology of hope builds upon and corrects certain deficiencies of Barth's theology.[13]

(5) Another point at which a chorus of voices has been raised against Barth relates to his rejection of the need for apologetic as opposed to dogmatic theology. Many critics accuse him of failing to relate Christian faith and theology to the questions and issues posed by the rising secular and scientific world view. Hence they find him most deficient at the point where nineteenth-century Protestant theology was strongest. They suggest that the only viable method for theology today is to address itself to the issues posed inside and outside the church by a secularism informed by modern science. Since Barth's theology failed to do this in any consistent fashion, his methodology must be rejected. It fosters an unhealthy and untenable dualism between faith and ordinary human experience. To continue with a dogmatics written for the church will encourage isolating the church from the world she is called to serve.[14]

POSTSCRIPT: BARTH AND THE THEOLOGY OF THE NINETEENTH CENTURY

A backward glance at the nineteenth-century Protestant theology from the vantage point of Barth's developed theology enables us to suggest several hypotheses concerning points of continuity and discontinuity.

(1) Barth's christocentric theology may be seen as the fulfillment of the attempts undertaken in this direction in the nineteenth century. In particular, Schleiermacher's desire to relate everything in the Christian faith to Jesus of Nazareth is realized far more radically by Barth than by Schleiermacher.

(2) In his own way Barth takes up the emphasis on the subjective appropriation of revelation in the nineteenth century. Barth contends that Schleiermacher need not have gone astray in beginning with man and the life of faith had he developed a true understanding of the work of the Holy Spirit.

He concludes, however, that the pious religious self-consciousness which describes itself is the alpha and omega of Schleiermacher's theology.[15]

(3) Barth's mature theological method is, in part, a response to Ludwig Feuerbach's taunt that "all theology is anthropology." Barth's christological dogmatics enables him to refer to true evangelical theology as "theoanthropology." That is, it is that theology "concerned with God as the God of *man*, but just for this reason, also with man as *God's* man."[16]

In conclusion, it can be affirmed that the final import of Barth's theology may well lie in the impetus he has given the church to concern herself first and last with the significance of him who is the center of her faith, namely, Jesus Christ. In a sense Barth has simply taken seriously the revelation of God in Jesus Christ which the church everywhere and at all times has acknowledged to be the center of her life and faith. In having caused us to listen anew to him who is the "same yesterday, today, and forever," Barth may have made his most lasting contribution.

Footnotes

CHAPTER I

1. Arnold B. Come, *An Introduction to Barth's "Dogmatics" for Preachers* (Philadelphia: The Westminster Press, 1963), p. 24.
2. Thomas F. Torrance, *Karl Barth: An Introduction to His Early Theology, 1910–1931* (London: SCM Press, 1962), p. 15.
3. Ibid., pp. 15-16.
4. Come, op. cit., p. 25.
5. Karl Barth, *Theology and Church: Shorter Writings, 1920–1928*, trans. Louise Pettibone Smith (New York: Harper & Row, 1962), p. 238. Cited hereafter as *TC*.
6. *TC*, p. 238.
7. *TC*, pp. 238-39.
8. Karl Barth, "Moderne Theologie und Reichsgottesarbeit," *Zeitschrift für Theologie und Kirche*, 19, no. 4 (1909), 319.
9. Karl Barth, "On Systematic Theology," *Scottish Journal of Theology*, 14, no. 3 (September, 1961), 225ff.
10. A good portion of this correspondence is available in *Revolutionary Theology in the Making: Barth-Thurneysen Correspondence, 1914–1925*, trans. James D. Smart (Richmond, Va.: John Knox Press, 1964). Cited hereafter as *Revolutionary Theology*.
11. Karl Barth, *The Word of God and the Word of Man*, trans. Douglas Horton (n.p., Pilgrim Press, 1928), p. 100. Cited hereafter as *WGWM*. This book was reprinted as a paperback in the Harper and Row Torchbook series.
12. Cited by Wilhelm Pauck, *Karl Barth: Prophet of a New Christianity?* (New York: Harper and Bros., 1931), p. 58.
13. *Revolutionary Theology*, p. 28.
14. *WGWM*, p. 34.
15. *WGWM*, p. 43.

16. Karl Barth, *The Epistle to the Romans*, trans. Edwyn C. Hoskyns from the sixth edition (London: Oxford University Press, 1933), p. 1. Cited hereafter as *Romans*.

17. *Romans*, p. 1.

18. *Romans*, p. 2. Reactions to the first and second editions of Barth's *Römerbrief* are available in *The Beginnings of Dialectical Theology*, vol. I., ed. James M. Robinson (Richmond, Va.: John Knox Press, 1968).

19. *Romans*, p. 10.

20. *Romans*, p. 7.

21. *WGWM*, p. 206.

22. Ibid.

23. Karl Barth, *Die christliche Dogmatik im Entwurf*. Vol. I. *Die Lehre vom Worte Gottes, Prolegomena zur christlichen Dogmatik* (Munich: Chr. Kaiser Verlag, 1927), pp. 456-57. Cited hereafter as *Christliche Dogmatik*.

24. Paul Tillich, "The Present Theological Situation in the Light of the Continental European Development," *Theology Today*, 6 (October, 1949), 302.

25. *Romans*, p. 31.

26. *Romans*, p. 316.

27. *Romans*, p. 30.

28. *Romans*, pp. 94-95.

29. Karl Barth and Eduard Thurneysen, *Komm Schöpfer Geist!* (Munich: Chr. Kaiser Verlag, 1924), p. 23.

30. *Romans*, p. 422.

31. *Romans*, p. 422.

32. *WGWM*, pp. 195-96.

33. *WGWM*, p. 98.

34. *WGWM*, p. 217.

35. Karl Barth, *Die Lehre von Gott, Die Kirchliche Dogmatik*, II/1 (Zollikon-Zurich: Evangelischer Verlag, 1948), p. 717. The German edition is cited hereafter as K.D. with appropriate volume numbers.

36. Karl Barth, "Abschied," *Zwischen den Zeiten*, 11, no. 6 (1933), 536.

37. *Revolutionary Theology*, p. 74.

38. Ibid., p. 203.

39. Heinrich Heppe, *Reformed Dogmatics* (London: George Allen & Unwin, Ltd.), p. v.

40. Ibid.

41. See Karl Barth, *How I Changed My Mind*, Introduction and Epilogue by John D. Godsey (Richmond, Va.: John Knox Press, 1966), p. 29.

42. *Christliche Dogmatik*, pp. vi-vii.

43. *TC*, note 1, p. 314.

44. *Christliche Dogmatik*, pp. 37-47.

45. Ibid., pp. 87-102.

46. Ibid., pp. 126-214.

47. Ibid., p. 111.

48. Karl Barth, *The Doctrine of the Word of God, Church Dogmatics*, I/1 (Edinburgh: T. & T. Clark, 1936), p. ix. The official English edition of *Church Dogmatics* is cited hereafter as C.D. with appropriate volume numbers.

49. *Christliche Dogmatik*, p. 403; cf. C.D. I/2, pp. 607-9, 728.

50. Ibid., p. 436.

51. Ibid., pp. 436-37.

52. Karl Barth, *Credo*, trans. J. Strathearn McNab (London: Hodder and Stoughton, 1936), p. 184.

53. *How I Changed My Mind*, pp. 42-43.

54. C.D. II/1, p. 4.

55. Karl Barth, *Anselm: Fides quaerens intellectum*, trans. I. W. Robertson (Cleveland: The World Publishing Co., 1962), p. 18. All citations from the English edition are cited hereafter as *Anselm*. Where I have used my translations from the German, I will use the symbol *FQI*.

56. *FQI*, pp. 13-14; cf. *Anselm*, p. 22.

57. *Anselm*, pp. 20-21.

58. *Anselm*, pp. 25-26.

59. For the thesis of Hans Urs von Balthasar, see his *The Theology of Karl Barth*, trans. John Drury (New York: Holt, Rinehart and Winston, 1971), pp. 43-150. Cited hereafter as Balthasar-*Barth*.

60. *Anselm*, pp. 29ff.; 117ff.

61. C.D. I/1, p. 25.

62. Regin Prenter, "Glaube and Erkennen bei Karl Barth," *Kerygma und Dogma*, 2, no. 3 (July, 1956), 178.

63. Cf. C.D. II/1, pp. 172ff. See Arthur C. Cochrane, *The Church's Confession Under Hitler* (Philadelphia: Westminster Press, 1962), for an analysis of this Confession in the church struggle in Germany; also Come, op. cit., pp. 51-56.

64. *How I Changed My Mind*, p. 57; see this series for Barth's reflections on these years.

65. C.D. IV/2, p. ix.

66. *How I Changed My Mind*, p. 71; see Barth's collection of sermons, *Deliverance to the Captives* (New York: Harper and Brothers, 1961).

67. *How I Changed My Mind*, pp. 71-72. Barth's bibliography contains 406 entries as of Dec. 1955. See the *Festschrift* honoring Barth on his seventieth birthday in 1956 entitled *Antwort*.

68. Karl Barth, *Evangelical Theology*, trans. Grover Foley (New York: Holt, Rinehart and Winston, 1963), p. xii-xiii. Cited hereafter as *ET*.

69. *ET*, p. xii.

70. See the foreword to *ET* for Barth's impressions of America.

71. Cf. C.D. IV/4, pp. viiff. for this and other statements relating to the completion of the C.D.

72. C.D. IV/4, pp. ix-x.

73. Statement by T. F. Torrance in C.D. IV/4, p. vi.

CHAPTER II

1. Cf. C.D. I/1, p. ix.
2. C.D. I/1, pp. 11-12.
3. C.D. II/2, p. 7.
4. C.D. IV/2, p. 122.
5. C.D. IV/1, p. 17.
6. C.D. I/2, p. 293.
7. C.D. I/1, p. 36.
8. Karl Barth, *The Humanity of God*, trans. T. Weiser and J. N. Thomas (Richmond, Va.: John Knox Press, 1960), pp. 12-14. Cited hereafter as *HG*.
9. *HG*, pp. 39-40.
10. C.D. I/1, p. 16.
11. C.D. I/1, p. 45.
12. Cf. esp. C.D. I/1, pp. 98-140.
13. *ET*, pp. 18-19.
14. C.D. I/1, p. 134.
15. *ET*, pp. 23-24.
16. *ET*, p. 26.
17. C.D. I/1, pp. 124-25.
18. C.D. II/1, p. 172.
19. C.D. I/1, p. 123.
20. C.D. I/2, p. 457; cf. pp. 457-740 for Barth's most extensive treatment of the doctrine of Holy Scripture. For a good summary, see *ET*, "The Witnesses," Part I, chapter 3.
21. C.D. I/2, p. 463.
22. C.D. I/2, p. 521.
23. C.D. I/2, p. 526.
24. C.D. I/2, p. 663; cf. pp. 459-60.
25. C.D. I/1, p. 51.
26. C.D. I/2, p. 743.
27. C.D. I/1, p. 61.
28. C.D. I/1, p. 75.

29. C.D. I/1, p. 106.
30. C.D. I/1, p. 136.
31. C.D. I/1, p. 136; cf. pp. 184-212.
32. Karl Barth, *God in Action: Theological Addresses,* trans. E. G. Homrighausen, et al. (New York: Round Table Press, 1936), pp. 11-12.
33. C.D. I/2, p. 5.
34. C.D. I/2, p. 3.
35. C.D. I/2, p. 5; cf. p. 819.
36. C.D. I/2, p. 5.
37. The best secondary treatments of Barth's doctrine of the Trinity are found in Claude Welch, *In This Name* (New York: Charles Scribner's Sons, 1952), and Robert W. Jenson, *God After God* (Indianapolis and New York: The Bobbs-Merrill Co., 1969).
38. C.D. I/1, p. v.
39. C.D. I/1, p. 339.
40. C.D. I/1, p. 334.
41. C.D. I/1, p. 348ff.
42. C.D. I/1, pp. 349-83.
43. C.D. I/1, p. 346.
44. C.D. I/1, p. 353.
45. C.D. I/1, p. 400.
46. C.D. I/1, p. 402.
47. C.D. I/1, p. 413.
48. Cf. C.D. I/1, pp. 423-31; for this entire discussion, see pp. 400-40.
49. C.D. I/1, p. 426.
50. C.D. I/1, pp. 439-40.
51. C.D. I/2, pp. 1-44; esp. pp. 3ff, 25ff.
52. C.D. I/2, p. 1.
53. C.D. I/2, p. 13.
54. C.D. I/2, p. 132. The basis of Barth's understanding of the Person of Jesus Christ and his christology is set forth in the section, "Very God and Very Man," C.D. I/2, pp. 132-71, and it takes the form of an exposition of John 1:1-14.
55. C.D. I/2, p. 25.
56. C.D. I/2, p. 27.
57. C.D. I/2, p. 29; for Barth's repeated emphasis upon the "hiddenness of God," see esp. C.D. I/1, pp. 184-212; C.D. II/1, pp. 179-204.
58. C.D. I/2, pp. 31f.
59. C.D. I/2, p. 33.
60. C.D. I/2, p. 33; cf. C.D. I/1, pp. 474-512.
61. C.D. I/2, p. 35.

62. K.D. II/1, p. 223.
63. C.D. I/2, p. 38.
64. C.D. I/2, pp. 39-40.
65. C.D. I/2, p. 45.
66. C.D. I/2, p. 101.
67. On this section, cf. C.D. I/2, pp. 45-121; Barth develops the implications of this christocentric reading of time for human existence in C.D. III/2, pp. 437-640.
68. C.D. III/2, p. 437.
69. C.D. I/2, p. 122.
70. C.D. I/2, p. 201.
71. C.D. I/2, p. 122; cf. pp. 172-202.
72. For Ritschl's approach, see the author's *An Introduction to the Theology of Albrecht Ritschl* (Philadelphia: The Westminster Press, 1969).
73. C.D. I/1, p. 227.
74. Cf. C.D. I/1, pp. 226-83.
75. C.D. I/2, p. 256; cf. pp. 250-57.
76. C.D. IV/1, p. 755.
77. C.D. IV/2, p. x.
78. C.D. I/2, p. 234; cf. pp. 232ff.
79. C.D. I/2, p. 236.
80. Cf. Karl Barth, "Rudolf Bultmann: Ein Versuch, ihn zu verstehen," *Theologische Studien,* no. 34 (1952).
81. C.D. IV/1, p. 249.
82. C.D. I/2, p. 257.
83. Cf. C.D. I/2, pp. 251ff.
84. C.D. I/2, p. 203.
85. C.D. I/2, pp. 203-32.
86. C.D. I/2, p. 242.
87. C.D. I/2, p. 222.
88. C.D. I/2, p. 233.
89. C.D. I/2, pp. 239-40.
90. C.D. I/2, p. 243.
91. C.D. I/2, pp. 242-79.
92. C.D. IV/2, pp. 125ff.
93. C.D. IV/2, p. 130.
94. C.D. IV/2, p. 129.
95. C.D. II/1, p. 3.
96. C.D. II/1, p. 13.
97. C.D. IV/1, pp. 645-46.
98. James Brown, *Subject and Object in Modern Theology* (New York: Macmillan Co., 1955), esp. pp. 140-67.
99. K.D. II/1, p. 14; cf. C.D. II/1, p. 14.

100. Cf. C.D. II/1, pp. 16ff.
101. C.D. IV/1, p. 742.
102. C.D. II/1, p. 22; cf. C.D. I/1, p. 25; *ET* on "Prayer," pp. 159-70.
103. C.D. I/1, pp. 233-39.
104. C.D. III/1, p. 349.
105. C.D. IV/1, p. 758.
106. C.D. IV/1, p. 758.
107. K.D. IV/1, pp. 854-55; C.D. IV/1, p. 764.
108. C.D. IV/1, pp. 776-79.
109. C.D. IV/1, p. 761.
110. C.D. IV/1, 760.
111. C.D. IV/1, pp. 617-27.
112. Cf. C.D. I/2, p. 280; C.D. II/1, pp. 204-54.
113. Karl Barth, *The Knowledge of God and the Service of God According to the Teaching of the Reformation,* trans. J. L. M. Haire and Ian Henderson (London: Hodder and Stoughton, 1955), p. 6.
114. C.D. II/1, pp. 27-29; 127ff; 172ff.
115. Karl Barth and Emil Brunner, *Natural Theology,* trans. Peter Frankel (London: The Centenary Press, 1946), p. 71.
116. C.D. II/1, p. 172.
117. C.D. II/1, p. 176.
118. C.D. II/1, p. 168.
119. C.D. II/1, p. 108.
120. C.D. II/1, pp. 98-110.
121. C.D. II/1, pp. 129-42.
122. C.D. II/1, p. 145.
123. C.D. II/1, p. 168.
124. C.D. II/1, pp. 142-78.
125. Cf. esp. C.D. II/1, pp. 63-128.
126. Cf. C.D. II/1, pp. 257-72.
127. Cf. C.D. I/1, pp. 260-83; C.D. II/1, the important section, "The Veracity of Man's Knowledge of God," pp. 204-54, for Barth's use of analogy.
128. C.D. II/1, pp. 216-23.
129. C.D. I/2, pp. 284-91.
130. C.D. I/2, p. 280.
131. C.D. I/2, pp. 299-300.
132. C.D. I/2, p. 303.
133. C.D. I/2, p. 280.
134. Herbert Hartwell, *The Theology of Karl Barth* (Philadelphia: The Westminster Press, 1964), pp. 87-88, is correct in calling attention to the fact that the German word, *Aufhebung,* can mean both "abolition" and "exaltation." This accounts for the fact—which many

interpreters miss—that Barth can speak of the revelation of God as the "judging but also reconciling presence of God in the world of human religion" (C.D. I/2, p. 280; pp. 325ff.).

135. C.D. I/2, p. 346. For a suggestive analysis of the problem of religion in modern theology, we refer to: Hendrik Kraemer, *Religion and the Christian Faith* (London: Lutterworth Press, 1956), esp. pp. 182-99.

CHAPTER III

1. C.D. II/1, p. 257.
2. C.D. II/1, par. 29-31.
3. C.D. II/1, p. 351.
4. C.D. II/1, p. 441.
5. C.D. II/1, pp. 272-321.
6. C.D. II/1, p. 261.
7. C.D. II/2, p. 5.
8. Hans Urs von Balthasar, *Karl Barth: Darstellung und Deutung seiner Theologie* (Cologne: Jakob Hegner Verlag, 1951), p. 187. Cf. Balthasar-*Barth*, p. 156.
9. K.D. II/2, p. 100; cf. C.D. II/2, p. 93.
10. C.D. II/2, p. 3.
11. C.D. II/2, p. 7.
12. C.D. II/2, pp. 7ff.
13. C.D. II/2, p. 77.
14. C.D. II/2, p. 3.
15. C.D. II/2, pp. 13ff.
16. See C.D. II/2, pp. 19-34, for points 5-6.
17. C.D. II/3, p. x.
18. C.D. II/2, p. 4.
19. C.D. II/2, p. 54.
20. On this section, see C.D. II/2, pp. 34-76.
21. C.D. II/2, p. 94.
22. E.g., Eph. 1:10, 23; 3:9; 1 Cor. 15:20; Col. 1:18; 2:10; Gal. 4:4; Heb. 1:2.
23. C.D. II/2, p. 94.
24. C.D. II/2, p. 95.
25. C.D. II/2, p. 100.
26. C.D. II/2, p. 101.
27. C.D. II/2, p. 103.
28. C.D. II/2, p. 94; cf. p. 104.
29. C.D. II/2, pp. 115-16.
30. K.D. II/2, p.124; cf. C.D. II/2, p. 116.
31. C.D. II/2, p. 101.

32. C.D. II/2, p. 116.
33. C.D. II/2, p. 117.
34. C.D. II/2, p. 118; cf. pp. 118ff.
35. C.D. II/2, p. 146.
36. C.D. II/2, pp. 145ff; see C.D. II/2, pp. 145-94, for Barth's rationale for his christological doctrine of predestination.
37. C.D. II/2, p. 161.
38. C.D. II/2, p. 162.
39. C.D. II/2, p. 123.
40. C.D. II/2, p. 125; on this section, see C.D. II/2, pp. 122ff., 161-68.
41. C.D. II/2, pp. 168-94.
42. C.D. II/2, p. 185.
43. C.D. II/2, pp. 196-97.
44. C.D. II/2, p. 198.
45. C.D. II/2, pp. 264-65.
46. C.D. II/2, p. 410.
47. C.D. II/2, p. 306; cf. pp. 306-409.
48. C.D. II/2, p. 419; cf. pp. 415ff. on universalism.
49. C.D. II/2, p. 450.
50. C.D. II/2, pp. 449-506.
51. C.D. III/1, p. 25; cf. C.D. III/1, par. 40 on this section.
52. C.D. III/1, p. 31; cf. esp. pp. 28ff.
53. C.D. III/1, pp. 42-329.
54. C.D. III/1, p. 44.
55. On this section, see C.D. III/1, pp. 228-329; also pp. 44ff.
56. C.D. III/1, p. 60.
57. C.D. III/1, p. 42.
58. C.D. III/1, p. 412; on this section, cf. pp. 330-414.
59. C.D. I/1, p. 148.
60. C.D. III/2, p. 19.
61. On this section, see C.D. III/2, pp. 2-132.
62. C.D. III/2, p. 3; Barth anticipated the direction of his christological anthropology in C.D. II/1, pp. 148-65.
63. C.D. III/2, p. ix.
64. C.D. III/2, pp. 55-71.
65. C.D. III/2, p. 132.
66. C.D. III/2, p. 68.
67. C.D. III/2, p. 69.
68. C.D. III/2, p. 69.
69. C.D. III/2, p. 70.
70. C.D. III/2, p. 70.
71. C.D. III/2, p. 135.
72. Barth says: "As an ontological determination of man in gen-

eral, the fact that among many others this One [i.e., the man, Jesus]
is also man means that we are men as in the person of this One we are
confronted by the divine Other" (C.D. III/2, p. 134).

73. C.D. III/2, p. 134.
74. C.D. III/2, p. 136.
75. C.D. III/2, p. 136.
76. C.D. III/2, p. 142.
77. C.D. III/2, p. 145.
78. C.D. III/2, pp. 142-47.
79. C.D. III/2, p. 142.
80. C.D. III/2, p. 149.
81. C.D. III/2, p. 149.
82. C.D. III/2, p. 150; on this section, see pp. 147-52.
83. C.D. III/2, p. 157.
84. C.D. III/2, p. 161.
85. C.D. III/2, p. 162.
86. C.D. III/2, p. 166.
87. C.D. III/2, p. 193.
88. On this section, see C.D. III/2, pp. 164-202.
89. Cf. C.D. III/2, par. 44-47.
90. C.D. III/2, p. 203.
91. C.D. III/2, p. 208.
92. C.D. III/2, p. 219.
93. C.D. III/2, p. 243.
94. C.D. III/2, p. 291.
95. On this section, see C.D. III/2, pp. 203-324; also, as early as
C.D. III/1, pp. 191f., Barth held that there was a certain likeness
between man and God in that both were relational beings. But Barth
distinguished this analogy (*analogia relationis*) from the analogy of
being; it does not provide the basis for a natural knowledge of God
by beginning with man.
96. C.D. IV/1, p. 3.
97. For Barth's schematic outline of this doctrine, see C.D. IV/1,
p. 79.
98. C.D. IV/1, p. 122.
99. C.D. IV/1, p. 123.
100. C.D. IV/1, p. 136.
101. C.D. IV/1, p. 125.
102. C.D. IV/1, p. 157.
103. C.D. IV/1, pp. 157-210.
104. C.D. IV/1, p. 215.
105. C.D. IV/1, p. 222.
106. C.D. IV/1, p. 223; for this section, see Barth's treatment of
"The Judge Judged in Our Place," C.D. IV/1, pp. 211-83.

107. C.D. IV/1, p. ix.

108. C.D. IV/1, p. 336; Barth's entire discussion is contra Bultmann.

109. C.D. IV/1, p. 296.

110. C.D. IV/1, p. 309; for Barth's extensive treatment of the resurrection see C.D. IV/1, pp. 283-357.

111. C.D. III/2, p. 34.

112. Cf. C.D. IV/1, pp. 358-513; C.D. IV/2, pp. 378-498; C.D. IV/3-I, pp. 368-478.

113. C.D. IV/1, pp. 360-61.

114. C.D. IV/1, p. 389.

115. C.D. IV/1, pp. 358-413, for Barth's christocentric approach.

116. On this section, see C.D. IV/1, pp. 413-78.

117. C.D. IV/1, p. 478.

118. C.D. IV/1, pp. 509-10.

119. For Barth's statement of the doctrine of original sin, see C.D. IV/1, pp. 499-513.

120. C.D. IV/1, p. 480; for this emphasis, cf. pp. 481-82, 492ff; C.D. IV/2, p. 488; cf. pp. 483ff. Earlier statements are in C.D. II/1, pp. 406ff.; C.D. III/1, pp. 189ff; C.D. III/2, p. 43; pp. 205ff.; 226ff.; 347ff.; C.D. III/3, pp. 58-90.

121. E.g., C.D. IV/1, p. 484.

122. K.D. III/2, p. 43; cf. C.D. III/2, p. 38. We have treated only one section of Barth's doctrine of sin—i.e., "The Pride and Fall of Man" contrasted with the "Lord Who Became a Servant." In subsequent sections of the doctrine of reconciliation, Barth contrasts the "Sloth and Misery of Man" with "Jesus Christ, the Servant as Lord" (C.D. IV/2, pp. 378-498). Finally, he treats "The Falsehood and Condemnation of Man" (C.D. IV/3-I, pp. 368-478) in light of "The Glory of the Mediator."

123. On "The Justification of Man," see C.D. IV/1, pp. 514-642. The best secondary treatment of Barth's doctrine of justification set forth within the context of his whole theology is the one by the Roman Catholic Hans Küng, *Justification: The Doctrine of Karl Barth and a Catholic Reflection*, trans. E. E. Tolk and D. Granskou (New York: Thomas Nelson and Sons, 1964).

124. C.D. IV/1, p. 514.

125. C.D. IV/1, p. 561.

126. C.D. IV/1, p. 549; cf. p. 555.

127. C.D. IV/1, p. 557.

128. C.D. IV/1, p. 604. Barth concludes each of the three major sections of the doctrine of reconciliation by analyzing in greater detail the manner in which the Holy Spirit is active in the (1) "Gathering" of the Christian community (C.D. IV/1), (2) the "Upbuilding" of

the Christian community (C.D. IV/2), and (3) the "Sending" of the Christian community (C.D. IV/3-II). Each of these is followed by a treatment of the work of the Holy Spirit in relationship to the individual in terms of (1) his faith (C.D. IV/1), (2) love (C.D. IV/2), and (3) hope (C.D. IV/3-II).

129. C.D. IV/2, p. 132; for this survey, see C.D. IV/2, pp. 3-154.

130. C.D. IV/2, pp. 180-81.

131. C.D. IV/2, p. 3; for Barth's treatment of this area, see C.D. IV/2, pp. 3-377.

132. C.D. IV/2, p. 503; the reader is referred to C.D. IV/2, pp. 499-511 for the relationship of justification and sanctification.

133. For the content of the doctrine of sanctification, see esp. C.D. IV/2, pp. 511-613.

134. C.D. IV/3-I, p. 3; see on this section, C.D. IV/3-I, pp. 3-165. On Barmen, cf. Chapter 1, note 63.

135. C.D. IV/3-I, pp. 165-274.

136. C.D. IV/3-I, pp. 274-367.

137. C.D. IV/3-II, p. 481.

138. On the "Vocation of Man," see C.D. IV/3-II, pp. 481-680; a good summary of the characteristics of Christian existence and the threats which afflict it is available in *ET*, pp. 63-196. (Parts II to IV).

139. C.D. IV/3-II, p. 681.

CHAPTER IV

1. Balthasar-*Barth*, p. 19. See also the important Catholic study of Barth by Küng, op. cit. For a valuable analysis of Barth's Catholic interpreters, see Grover E. Foley, "The Catholic Critics of Karl Barth," *Scottish Journal of Theology*, 14, no. 2 (1961), 136-55.

2. Balthasar-*Barth*, p. 19. In 1970 a separate volume (K.D. *Registerband*, ed. Helmut Krause) indexing (1) all of the biblical references, (2) all of the important subjects, and (3) names in the K.D. was published. In addition over 355 pages of exegetical and expository materials are extracted from the K.D. and arranged in accordance with the liturgical calendar. It is to be hoped that an English translation of this index volume will be forthcoming.

3. C.D. I/2, p. 293.

4. C.D. I/2, p. 21.

5. For a good statement of Barth's position, see *ET*, chaps. 3-4; an analysis of Barth's position by Friedrich-Wilhelm Marquardt is available in K.D. *Registerband*.

6. K.D. *Registerband*, p. vi. For Barth's early statements on the relationship of theology and preaching, see *WGWM*. Most secondary studies also deal with this emphasis, e.g., *Antwort*.

7. See Robert W. Jenson's *God After God* for a careful analysis of the strengths and weaknesses of Barth's doctrine of God.

8. Thomas C. Oden, *The Promise of Barth* (Philadelphia and New York: J. B. Lippincott Co., 1969), p. 37. This is a brief and helpful English introduction to Barth's ethics.

9. *HG*, p. 55; this essay provides a good summary of Barth's Christian and christological humanism.

10. *Romans*, p. 314; for an analysis of Barth's eschatology, see Jürgen Moltmann, *The Theology of Hope*, trans. James W. Leitch (New York: Harper and Row, 1967), esp. pp. 37-58.

11. For this criticism, see esp. Balthasar-*Barth*, pp. 151-203; Come, op. cit., pp. 130-67.

12. Moltmann, op. cit., p. 100.

13. Cf. Moltmann, op. cit., esp. pp. 37-50; see also Jenson, *God After God*, pp. 139-93, for a critique of Barth's doctrine of God and the author's suggestive proposals.

14. For one of the most perceptive critiques of Barth and neoorthodoxy, see Langdon Gilkey, *Naming the Whirlwind: The Renewal of God-Language* (Indianapolis and New York: Bobbs-Merrill Co., 1969), esp. pp. 73-106.

15. Karl Barth, *Protestant Thought: From Rousseau to Ritschl*, trans. B. Cozens and H. Hartwell (New York: Harper & Bros., 1959), p. 344.

16. *ET*, pp. 11-12.

Selected Bibliography

Barth's complete bibliography numbers over 500 books, articles, sermons, and papers. Ch. von Kirschbaum compiled a complete bibliography of Barth's writings up to December, 1955, for the volume *Antwort* in honor of Barth's seventieth birthday. In a volume marking Barth's eightieth birthday in 1960, *Parrhesia*, Eberhard Busch has added Barth's writings up to that date. Both lists include some of the translations of Barth's works into foreign languages.

This bibliography includes a brief list of some of the important writings of Barth and studies of him available in English. Barth's *Faith of the Church* (New York: Meridian Books, World Publishing Company, 1958), contains an extensive bibliography of Barth's writings translated into English.

I. WORKS BY KARL BARTH

Ad Limina Apostolorum: An Appraisal of Vatican II. Translated by Keith R. Crim. Richmond, Va.: John Knox Press, 1968.

Against the Stream: Shorter Post-War Writings, 1946–52. Edited by Ronald Gregor Smith. New York: Philosophical Library, 1954.

Anselm: Fides quaerens intellectum. Translated by Ian W. Robertson. Cleveland: The World Publishing Co., 1962.

Christ and Adam: Man and Humanity in Romans 5. Translated by T. A. Smail. New York: Harper & Bros., 1957.

Church Dogmatics. Edited by G. W. Bromiley and T. F. Torrance. Edinburgh: T. & T. Clark, 1936-1969.

I/1. *The Doctrine of the Word of God.* Prolegomena, Part 1. Translated by G. T. Thomson, 1936.

I/2. *The Doctrine of the Word of God.* Prolegomena, Part 2. Translated by G. T. Thomson and H. Knight, 1956.

II/1. *The Doctrine of God,* Part 1. Translated by T. H. L. Parker, W. B. Johnston, H. Knight, J. L. M. Haire, 1957.

II/2. *The Doctrine of God,* Part 2. Translated by G. W. Bromiley, J. C. Campbell, Iain Wilson, J. Strathearn McNab, H. Knight, R. A. Stewart, 1957.

III/1. *The Doctrine of Creation,* Part 1. Translated by J. W. Edwards, O. Bussey, H. Knight, 1958.

III/2. *The Doctrine of Creation,* Part 2. Translated by H. Knight. G. W. Bromiley, J. K. S. Reid, R. H. Fuller, 1960.

III/3. *The Doctrine of Creation,* Part 3. Translated by G. W. Bromiley, R. Ehrlich, 1961.

III/4. *The Doctrine of Creation,* Part 4. Translated by A. T. Mackay, T. H. L. Parker, H. Knight, H. A. Kennedy, J. Marks, 1961.

IV/1. *The Doctrine of Reconciliation,* Part 1. Translated by G. W. Bromiley, 1956.

IV/2. *The Doctrine of Reconciliation,* Part 2. Translated by G. W. Bromiley, 1958.

IV/3. *The Doctrine of Reconciliation,* Part 3, vols. i and ii. Translated by G. W. Bromiley, 1961, 1962.

IV/4. *The Doctrine of Reconciliation,* Part 4. Translated by G. W. Bromiley, 1969.

Church Dogmatics: A Selection. Introduction by Helmut Gollwitzer. Translated and edited by G. W. Bromiley. New York: Harper & Row, 1962.

Community, State, and Church. Introduction by Will Herberg. Garden City, N. Y.: Doubleday and Co., 1960.

Deliverance to the Captives. Translated by M. Weiser. New York: Harper & Bros., 1959.

Dogmatics in Outline. Translated by G. T. Thomson. New York: Harper & Bros., 1959.

Evangelical Theology: An Introduction. Translated by Grover Foley. New York: Holt, Rinehart and Winston, 1963. (It is also published in paperback as a Doubleday Anchor Book.)

How I Changed My Mind. Introduction and Epilogue by John D. Godsey. Richmond, Va.: John Knox Press, 1966.

How to Serve God in a Marxist Land (with Johannes Hamel). New York: Association Press, 1959.

The Humanity of God. Translated by J. N. Thomas and T. Weiser. Richmond, Va.: John Knox Press, 1960.

Karl Barth's Table Talk. Edited by John D. Godsey. Richmond, Va.: John Knox Press, 1963.

The Knowledge of God and the Service of God, According to the Teaching of the Reformation. Translated by J. M. L. Haire and Ian Henderson. London: Hodder and Stoughton, 1949.

Natural Theology; comprising "Nature and Grace" by Professor Dr. Emil Brunner and the reply "No!" by Dr. Karl Barth. Translated by Peter Frankel. London: The Centenary Press, 1946.

Protestant Thought: From Rousseau to Ritschl. Translated by B. Cozens and H. Hartwell. New York: Harper & Bros., 1959.

Revolutionary Theology in the Making: Barth-Thurneysen Correspondence, 1914–1925. Translated by James D. Smart. Richmond, Va.: John Knox Press, 1964.

The Teaching of the Church Regarding Baptism. Translated by Ernest A. Payne. London: SCM Press, 1948.

Theology and Church: Shorter Writings, 1920–1928. Translated by Louise Pettibone Smith. New York: Harper & Row, 1962.

II. WORKS ABOUT KARL BARTH

BALTHASAR, HANS URS VON. *The Theology of Karl Barth.* Translated by John Drury. New York: Holt, Rinehart and Winston, 1971.

BERKOUWER, G. C. *The Triumph of Grace in the Theology of Karl Barth.* Translated by Harry R. Boer. Grand Rapids: Wm. B. Eerdmans, 1956.

BROWN, JAMES. *Subject and Object in Modern Theology.* New York: The Macmillan Company, 1955.

CASALIS, GEORGES. *Portrait of Karl Barth.* Translated with an Introduction by Robert McAfee Brown. Garden City: Doubleday & Co., 1963.

COME, ARNOLD B. *An Introduction to Barth's Dogmatics for Preachers.* Philadelphia: The Westminster Press, 1963.

DILLENBERGER, JOHN. *God Hidden and Revealed.* Philadelphia: Muhlenberg Press, 1953.

HARTWELL, HERBERT. *The Theology of Karl Barth: An Introduction.* Philadelphia: The Westminster Press, 1964.

JENSON, ROBERT W. *Alpha and Omega: A Study in the Theology of Karl Barth.* New York: Thomas Nelson, 1963.

————. *God After God.* Indianapolis: Bobbs-Merrill Co., 1969.

KÜNG, HANS. *Justification: The Doctrine of Karl Barth and a Catholic Reflection.* Introduction by Karl Barth. Translated by E. E. Tolk and D. Granskou. New York: Thomas Nelson & Sons, 1964.

MACKINTOSH, HUGH ROSS. *Types of Modern Theology: Schleiermacher to Barth.* New York: Charles Scribner's Sons, 1937.

ODEN, THOMAS C. *The Promise of Barth: The Ethics of Freedom.* Philadelphia: J. B. Lippincott Co., 1969.

ROBINSON, JAMES M., ed. *The Beginnings of Dialectical Theology,* vol. I. Translated by Keith R. Crim, et al. Richmond, Va.: John Knox Press, 1968.

SMART, JAMES D. *The Divided Mind of Modern Theology: Karl Barth and Rudolf Bultmann, 1908–1933.* Philadelphia: The Westminster Press, 1967.

TORRANCE, THOMAS F. *Karl Barth: An Introduction to His Early Theology, 1910–1931.* London: SCM Press, 1962.

WEBER, OTTO. *Karl Barth's Church Dogmatics.* An Introductory Report on vols. I/1 to III/4. Translated by Arthur C. Cochrane. Philadelphia: The Westminster Press, 1953.

WELCH, CLAUDE. *In This Name.* New York: Charles Scribner's Sons, 1952.

WINGREN, GUSTAF. *Theology in Conflict.* Translated by E. H. Wahlstrom. Philadelphia: Muhlenberg Press, 1968.

WOLF, ERNST; VON KIRSCHBAUM, CH.; FREY, RUDOLF; editors. *Antwort: Karl Barth zum siebzigsten Geburtstag.* Zollikon-Zurich: Evangelischer Verlag, 1956.